100
GREATEST TRIPS

**TRAVEL
+LEISURE**

The courtyard at Mas des Lauriers, a farmhouse for rent near Aix-en-Provence, France.

TRAVEL +LEISURE

100
GREATEST TRIPS

FROM THE EDITORS OF THE WORLD'S
LEADING TRAVEL MAGAZINE

FOURTH EDITION

TRAVEL +LEISURE
BOOKS

AMERICAN EXPRESS PUBLISHING CORPORATION
NEW YORK

TRAVEL + LEISURE
100 GREATEST TRIPS FOURTH EDITION

For T+L
Editor Irene Edwards
Assistant Book Editor Alison Goran
Associate Managing Editor Laura Teusink
Photo Coordinator Nicole Schilit
Reporters Lisa Cheng, Jennifer Flowers, Catesby Holmes, Sarah Kantrowitz, Stirling Kelso, Peter Jon Lindberg, Kathryn O'Shea-Evans, Bree Sposato
Copy Editor Diego Hadis
Researchers Bradford Taylor, John Wogan

For DK
Editorial Lead Heather Jones
Senior Art Editor Ann Cannings
DTP Designer David McDonald
Senior Production Controller Rachel Lloyd
Associate Publisher Nigel Duffield

TRAVEL + LEISURE
Editor-in-Chief Nancy Novogrod
Creative Director Nora Sheehan
Executive Editor Jennifer Barr
Deputy Editor Laura Begley
Managing Editor Mike Fazioli
Arts/Research Editor Mario R. Mercado
Senior Copy Editor Kathy Roberson
Photo Director Katie Dunn
Production Director Rosalie Abatemarco Samat
Production Manager Ayad Sinawi

AMERICAN EXPRESS PUBLISHING CORPORATION
President, C.E.O. Ed Kelly
S.V.P., Chief Marketing Officer Mark V. Stanich
C.F.O., S.V.P., Corporate Development & Operations Paul B. Francis
V.P., General Managers Keith Strohmeier, Frank Bland
V.P., Books & Products Marshall Corey
Director, Book Programs Bruce Spanier
Senior Manager Branded Books Eric Lucie
Assistant Manager Branded Books Lizabeth Clark
Director of Fulfillment & Premium Value Phil Black
Manager of Customer Experience & Product Development Charles Graver
Director of Finance Tom Noonan
Associate Business Manager Uma Mahabir
Operations Director Anthony White

Cover design by Wendy Scofield
Cover photograph by Martin Morrell

ISBN 9780756659929
ISSN 1933-1231

Published by American Express Publishing Corporation
1120 Avenue of the Americas, New York, New York 10036
With Contributions and Distributed by DK Publishing, Inc.
375 Hudson Street, New York, New York 10014

Manufactured in China

The Colony Glacier, near the Alyeska Resort, in Girdwood, Alaska.

CONTENTS

The lookout near Chatham Light, in Cape Cod, Massachusetts.

INTRODUCTION

BY NANCY NOVOGROD, EDITOR-IN-CHIEF

As every seasoned traveler knows, a great journey is not about how far one goes or how many places one visits, but about the small, intimate, unforgettable encounters along the way. Even the most epic adventures come down to single moments, and it's invariably these that we remember best: the vividly colored produce at the farmer's market in Aix-en-Provence; the whirl of a spinning wheel in Tangier; the perfect trout caught on Idaho's Snake River; the sight of a Balinese family on the beach, setting prayer baskets afloat on the tide.

For 38 years, *Travel + Leisure* magazine has been devoted to seeking out those very moments—and this book is a celebration of that quest. For the fourth edition of our annual *100 Greatest Trips* series, my editors and I culled from thousands of journeys and destinations featured in T+L and its six foreign editions over the past year. Our goal: to collect a wide-ranging and diverse array of travel ideas, organized by region, that we hope will coax you to follow our lead—or perhaps fashion a greatest trip of your own. To help get you started, you'll find a comprehensive Guide section with maps and an up-to-date directory of hotels, restaurants, shops, museums, and more.

The journeys and places we selected range from the *au courant* (the scintillating nightlife in Bangkok; a burgeoning design scene in Cape Town) to the timeless (a medieval castle tour on the Rhine, or a steamship cruise down the Nile). Some destinations—such as Italy's untrammeled Cilento Coast, and the tiny Caribbean island of Bequia—are making their debut appearance in the *Greatest Trips* series. Others may be more familiar, but have

lately been reinvented or re-energized: the suddenly trendy Cotswolds; a new and virtually unrecognizable Delhi. Some are far-flung (the Marquesas, the Andes), while a few may lie just down the road (Cape Cod, Tucson, Seattle).

Seeking a quiet, rejuvenating retreat? Consider a trip to a tranquil *ryokan* in Japan, or to the garden villas of Lake Como. Or perhaps it's outsize drama you're after? Turn to Scotland's wild and rugged Isle of Skye, or to the epic, dream-inspiring deserts of Namibia. Whatever your passion and preference, you'll find a journey that fits—from idyllic beaches in Anguilla, Brazil, and Bora-Bora to culinary adventures in Tokyo, Melbourne, and Madrid. Thrilling drives in New Zealand, Ireland, Nevada, and coastal Maine. A wine-lover's odyssey in Portugal's Douro Valley; a barbecue quest in Memphis. Insider guides to the newest style havens, from Los Angeles to London to Istanbul. Wildlife encounters in Belize, Baja, and Malaysia. Even a tour of the quieter, gentler, romantic side of Manhattan.

What's more, many of these journeys are eminently affordable—a summer idyll on the Jersey Shore, an antiques quest in Minnesota, even a gourmand's tour of Paris, where great value can be found at some of the city's top restaurants.

The main purpose of this book is quite simple: to inspire you to travel. To open your mind to new experiences; to get you to engage with the world and enhance not only your own life but the lives of those you encounter. We at T+L believe firmly in the transformative power of travel—which is not only good for you, it's good for the world as well.

Lifeguards at the ready at Stegar's Beach, in Cape May, New Jersey.

UNITED STATES
+CANADA

A buoy-laden shack near Cape Neddick, left. Below: Lobster bisque at Blue Sky, in York Beach.

MAINE'S SOUTHERN COAST

Pine forests meet the spray of the surf

WILDLIFE SANCTUARIES AND SKEE-BALL ARCADES, roadside farm stands and seaside snack bars, beaches with actual sand (sand!): the southern coast is Maine at its most alluring. There's an enduring authenticity to this corner of New England, which never feels overrun with visitors, even in summer. And no, that gas station attendant is not putting you on with his accent; like southern Maine itself, he's the genuine article.

The perfect driving route begins right over the New Hampshire border with the town of Kittery and its tranquil residential enclaves—woodsy Kittery Point has the Chauncey Creek Lobster Pier and a virtually undiscovered state park, Fort Foster. Just up the coast are the Yorks: Rockwellian York Village, blue-blooded York Harbor, and honky-tonk York Beach, where old-time motels, ice cream parlors, and an arcade share the sand with the refined Blue Sky restaurant. Off nearby Cape Neddick stands whitewashed Nubble Light, the state's most celebrated lighthouse.

A long-standing artists' haven, Ogunquit has an impressive dining scene and the loveliest beach on the coast. Walk the oceanfront Marginal Way footpath to MC Perkins Cove, a restaurant on a marina traversed by a pedestrian-only wooden drawbridge. Up the coast, Kennebunkport (along with its sister village, Kennebunk) has long been an upper-class enclave—a heritage reinforced by a stay at the discreet Hidden Pond or the gracious Captain Lord Mansion. But for all the patrician polish, the "K'bunks" retain a salty flavor, best savored in the many lobster shacks lining the shore. +

For The Guide, see page 262.

Dunes at Race Point Beach, with the Life Saving Station at Provincetown in the distance.

CAPE COD

The iconic American summer vacation

DRIVING ACROSS THE CAPE COD CANAL—the thin strip of water that separates the 70-mile-long peninsula from mainland Massachusetts—is like leaving the real world behind. A vacation on Cape Cod is all about simple pleasures and the joys of endless summer. Life hasn't changed much in decades, thanks in part to the locals (Cape Codders are a fiercely protective bunch). There may be a Marc Jacobs boutique in Provincetown, but the longtime shell shop remains tucked behind the saltwater taffy store. And despite the influx of big money in Chatham, the town band still plays in the park on summer Friday nights, and fire trucks still lumber down Main Street in the annual Fourth of July parade.

Jutting out into the Atlantic Ocean like a crooked arm making a fist, Cape Cod is made up of four distinct regions: Upper, Mid-, Lower, and Outer. Upper Cape has Sandwich, the Cape's oldest and most historic town, as well as boutique-lined Falmouth and the little fishing town of Woods Hole.

Mid-Cape includes Hyannis, that famous Kennedy enclave, which acts as Cape Cod's big city. The best-known town in the Lower Cape is Chatham, home to the Chatham Bars Inn (opened in 1914, and still the area's toniest address). Great lobster rolls can be found 10 miles north in the town of Orleans, where Cap't Cass Rock Harbor Seafood proves that at the best joints, the menu doesn't vary much: fried, fried, and more fried. The funky BYOB has wood floors, shelves lined with old seashells, handwritten menus taped to the walls, and colorful buoys covering the exterior. For the Cape's most fashionable boutique, head to

Clockwise from top left: A lobster roll at Cap't Cass Rock Harbor Seafood, in Orleans; the Shell Shop, Provincetown; rugs at Periwinkle, in Wellfleet; kids' clothing at Weekend, in Orleans.

Weekend, where former set designer Mari Porcari sells floral-print organic quilts, colorful summer dresses, and eco-friendly bamboo bowls in an 1835 general store with lime green walls.

The Outer Cape stretches from the western side of the peninsula bordering Cape Cod Bay to the protected Atlantic beaches of the Cape Cod National Seashore. In Wellfleet, a longtime magnet for artists and (curiously) psychotherapists, Periwinkle is the go-to place for brightly colored plates, napkins, glassware, and rugs. Sample some of the Cape's best seafood at Wicked Oyster, and pick up a jar of beach plum jelly or rose hip jam at Briar Lane Jams & Jellies, an open-air stand on the side of the highway.

Last stop: Provincetown, also called P-town, a haven for gay men and women, artists and writers, fishermen and whale-watchers. A beaded mermaid curtain sets the tone at the kitschy Shell Shop, which has supplied beach houses on the Cape with shell-encrusted mirrors and starfish since 1978. At the neon-lit, often-photographed Lobster Pot, order the lobster as God intended it—steamed, with drawn butter on the side. +

For The Guide, see page 262.

The Lobster Pot, a Provincetown institution.

BLOCK ISLAND

New England's lesser-known beach retreat

THIRTEEN MILES OFF THE COAST of Rhode Island, "the Block," as locals call it, is a fraction of the size of Nantucket and Martha's Vineyard—and far less discovered. The appeal lies in its simplicity: small-town New England set against an Andrew Wyeth–worthy landscape, with only 1,000 year-round residents. Weathered saltbox cottages are huddled behind windswept dunes, and 200 miles of colonial-era stone walls cut across fields that end in 250-foot rocky cliffs. Nearly 40 percent of the land is designated as a nature preserve; an extensive network of hiking trails leads to secret beaches and freshwater lily ponds. (You can hike the entire perimeter in approximately eight hours.)

Biking is another good way to explore the island, thanks to stretches of flat terrain that run along the shore. Grab your wheels near the ferry at Aldo's Mopeds and Bikes, then stop at the pint-size Three Sisters in Old Harbor, where founding sibling Brigid Price whips up her signature sandwiches for worn-out cyclists.

At Three Sisters sandwich shop, below. Right, from top: Baked oysters with spinach at Eli's Restaurant; the Victorian-style Hotel Manisses. Opposite: A dock at New Harbor, as seen from the Oar Restaurant.

Block Island has plenty of houses to rent—from renovated old country barns to contemporary cabins with ocean views. At the creaky 138-year-old Hotel Manisses, named for one of the island's original settlers, the 16 rooms are decorated with floral wallpaper and antique furniture. Down the hill in a gray clapboard cottage is Eli's Restaurant, serving up soft-shell crab over fresh pasta. On the southern side of Great Salt Pond, the veranda at the casual Oar Restaurant has the best view of New Harbor, which fills up with moored sailboats at dusk. +

For The Guide, see page 262.

HUDSON RIVER VALLEY

Historic towns reborn

A weekend afternoon on Warren Street, in downtown Hudson.

The goods at Paper Trail, a stationery and gift shop in Rhinebeck, left. Below: The day's menu at Mercato, in Red Hook.

JUST LIKE RIP VAN WINKLE, the region's most famous literary son, the Hudson Valley has emerged from a deep slumber. New galleries, performance spaces, and restaurants have joined the landmark mansions and mom-and-pop stores; residents now run the gamut from farmers to art-world heavy hitters (was that Brice Marden at the neighborhood tavern?).

Start at the northern end in the small city of Hudson, where there's scarcely a vacant space left on Warren Street. Spend a lazy afternoon antiquing and browsing the 12,000-plus volumes at Hudson City Books before heading to DABA restaurant for Swedish meatballs and elk carpaccio.

Farther downriver, in Annandale-on-Hudson, the Frank Gehry–designed Fisher Center for the Performing Arts landed like a meteor on the Bard College campus, its rippling sheets of stainless steel startling and spectacular amid a landscape still dominated by farms, stone walls, and Calvert Vaux cottages. Nearby villages Tivoli, Red Hook, and Rhinebeck are abuzz with whimsical boutiques and fun places to eat, such as Italian osteria Mercato and the burger-centric Terrapin Red Bistro. The bar at Tivoli's Madalin Hotel serves as Hudson Valley's social hot spot.

Even before the arrival of Dia: Beacon in 2003, artists were already homing in on Beacon as an affordable alternative to New York City, but the opening of the contemporary art venue turned the working-class town into an essential destination on the international art map. As befits the so-called Brooklyn North, galleries—more than 10 on Main Street alone—dominate the brick storefronts; and Homespun Foods, the friendly coffee joint, percolates all day long. +

For The Guide, see page 263

NEW YORK CITY

Quiet nooks in the urban jungle

Salon de Ning, at the Peninsula New York, above. Opposite: The Oak Bar in the Plaza Hotel.

LOST AMID MIDTOWN'S INCESSANT BUZZ, enveloped by multitudes, it's hard to imagine this was once a chestnut and oak tree–swathed isle. But serenity can still be found here, in intimate pockets—you just have to know where to look. Find a tranquil seat at the newly spruced-up Oak Bar, the Plaza Hotel's watering hole, where the wood paneling glows warmly and the Central Park views are as magical as ever. Three blocks south, the Peninsula New York's new rooftop bar, Salon de Ning, channels 1930's Shanghai with silk pillow–laden daybeds and cocktails of passion fruit, lychee liqueur, and mint. Two blocks off Union Square, behind an unmarked door, lies the Inn at Irving Place—an Edith Wharton–era town house turned hotel where a five-course tea service starts at noon on weekends.

In the leafy West Village, Café Cluny is like a portal to a Gallic village (where waitresses sport Audrey Tatou pigtails). And at Smith & Mills—the tiniest boîte in TriBeCa, if not the entire East Coast—the cozy banquettes can accommodate only a dozen-odd patrons, who linger until 3 a.m. nursing Sazeracs and slurping Malpeques. Bright lights, big city? From this vantage point, New York feels like the smallest town on earth. +

For The Guide, see page 263.

JERSEY SHORE

The unexpected joys of the underdog state

A produce stand at Viking Village in Barnegat Light, one of the many seaside commnities along the Jersey Shore, above. Opposite: Brothers Ted (far left) and Matt Lee pedal on Viking Village's boardwalk.

THERE'S A MESMERIZING, Super 8–film quality to the perfect beach day, when the air is gelatin-smooth and the sun flickers off the water. On a narrow strip of Brant Beach, New Jersey, kids on skimboards surf the shallows of the Atlantic while their younger siblings splash in the gullies. A vintage 1960's Good Humor ice cream truck idles in the distance. You've never tasted a Creamsicle so sublime.

The history of American leisure has its beginnings on the Jersey Shore, where the nostalgic beach vacation still endures. Cape May, the nation's first seaside resort, is also one of its best-preserved Victorian districts, with crape myrtles sprouting from the sidewalks and American-flag bunting hanging from porches laden with rockers and wicker furniture. Settle into a cabana on the sand in front of Congress Hall, the town's buttercup yellow grand hotel, reopened in 2002 by ex-Helmsley tycoons Curtis Bashaw and Craig Wood. (The clutch of inns and rooms they've developed in the last decade are the most attractive offerings in town.) Duck into the Virginia Hotel for a quick drink and appetizers at the Ebbitt Room, whose cheeky style—Louis XIV chairs in white

Clockwise from top left: Ariel Smith, granddaughter of a local lifeguard, in Cape May; the Lobster House; a cabana at Cape May's Congress Hall hotel; a vacationing family on Long Beach Island.

crocodile leather—invites the question: Does Cape May need foie gras? The answer is no, but you won't mind polishing off the pistachio-dusted scallops and the impressive cheese plate nonetheless. Fulfill those cravings for sea critters and beer at the Lobster House, on one of the fishing docks that hug the bay side of town; arrive at 8:45 p.m. and you'll have no competition for a seat at the handsome bar or the undivided attention of the professional, white-jacketed bartenders. Order oysters on the half shell, chilled blue crab, and cold Flying Fish beers.

Map a lazy route north past the 1950's-era motels of Wildwood and the casinos of Atlantic City to Long Beach Island—a strip of sand just a few blocks wide and 18 miles long, linked by a causeway to the Jersey mainland. The genial stores and attractions that dot Long Beach Boulevard, with names like the Sand Trap and Things A Drift, are the lifeblood of this place. Walk the sandy block of picturesque shore cottages to the ocean, where you can bask in the true genius of the Jersey Shore—an unapologetically weird, wonderful concoction of old and new. +

For The Guide, see page 263.

Chef Michael Glatz's "sushi pizza," below.
Right: The historic Hotel Fauchère.

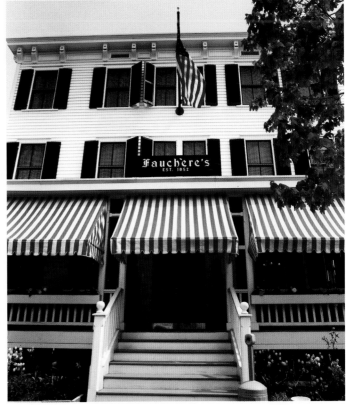

MILFORD

The comeback kid

FROM THE TOP OF THE KNOB—a 400-foot bluff that towers above one end of Broad Street, the main thoroughfare—you can see all of Milford, a comely village of tree-lined streets and handsome Victorians. This northeastern Pennsylvania town is like a Currier & Ives print come to life. In the late 18th century, Milford's scenic beauty and pure air brought an affluent crowd of vacationers, some of whom built weekend homes created by the leading architects of their day. (The magnificent Grey Towers, designed by Richard Morris Hunt, sits high on a hill at the edge of town, and is now an arts and conservation center open to visitors.) The golden age lasted until World War II; when Americans took to faster cars and the new interstate highways, the tourist trade began to slacken. As far as the outside world was concerned, Milford all but slipped out of sight.

Recently, Milford residents have revived some of the town's old luster. After five years of painstaking work, the Hotel Fauchère—founded in 1852 by Louis Fauchère, master chef at New York City's Delmonico's restaurant—reopened. Bright-striped awnings now shade its front porch, and the hallways display paintings by Hudson River School artists. In the restaurant, chef Michael Glatz interprets Louis Fauchère's dishes, adding a few creations of his own. Among them: "sushi pizza," made with tuna tartare, flying-fish eggs, and a crust of tempura-fried rice. Downstairs, the informal Bar Louis draws a regular gathering of Milfordians and visitors who compare notes on life, past and present, in this East Coast idyll. +

For The Guide, see page 263.

PIEDMONT REGION

Haute inns and an emerging wine country

EAST OF THE BLUE RIDGE MOUNTAINS, Virginia's Piedmont is in many ways still the same rural paradise that captivated Thomas Jefferson and James Monroe—only now it lures the likes of John Grisham and Robert Duvall. Country lanes wind through villages of trim clapboard houses and around pastures framed by white fences. And even though progressive farms and serious wineries have blossomed, life continues at a blissfully slow pace.

Tucked away from busy Route 211, tiny Washington has a bygone charm, with neat-as-a-pin brick buildings that seem out of a period movie. The Inn at Little Washington's well-heeled crowd has helped turn the community into an impressive hotbed of culture, with two theaters and a clutch of excellent galleries. Half an hour south lies Culpeper, whose Main Street district has gone from rundown Americana relic to lively commercial hub. Out in the country, serious vintners—among them the bucolic White Hall Vineyards, the

The 1804 Inn at Barboursville Vineyards, below.
Right, from top: A guest room at the Inn at Little
Washington; at Mountfair Vineyards, in Crozet.
Opposite: The landscape outside Madison.

Italian-owned Barboursville Vineyards, and the recently opened Mountfair Vineyards—have taken Virginia wine making from novelty act to serious pursuit.

Moseying speed is best for sampling the down-home appeal of the area's small burgs. On a stroll through Madison, you'll find front porches meant for lingering and an old church converted into a bustling quilt shop. In contrast, Charlottesville may best be known as home to the University of Virginia, but the thriving mini-metropolis has fashionable shops (like the Warehouse District's Georgie) and restaurants (the industrial-chic Mas), along with an arts scene to wow the most sophisticated urbanite. Much of the action revolves around the pedestrian mall, where a free-speech monument—a massive slate wedge, with chalk for passersby to scrawl their thoughts—was just unveiled in front of city hall. Our founding fathers would be proud. ✦

For The Guide, see page 263.

ASHEVILLE

A forward-thinking mountain town

IMAGINE A PLACE where the local paper advertises an "organic mechanic," the streets teem with bandana-wearing banjo players, and tempeh is common on menus—and you have the bucolic Southern retreat of Asheville. Encircled by the rolling Blue Ridge Mountains, the North Carolina town has been luring travelers in search of a holistic holiday since the late 19th century. "The allure of Asheville is that it's quaint but also becoming more cosmopolitan," says Alicia Sessoms, who moved here from Brooklyn five years ago to open Table Restaurant with her chef husband, Jacob. To dress up the warehouse-like space, Alicia gathers flowers for the

Duck confit with glazed carrots, roasted brussel sprouts, and figs at Table Restaurant.

Clockwise from top left: A server at Early Girl Eatery; local honey for sale at an outdoor market; the hilltop Black Walnut Bed & Breakfast.

hand-hewn maple tables, while Jacob cooks up dishes like bucatini with fresh snap peas and pancetta with produce sourced from nearby farms. Homegrown ingredients are given equal billing at casual brunch favorite Early Girl Eatery, where lines snake out the door for Southern standards such as fried green tomatoes and shrimp and grits.

The combination of progressive vibe and rural setting has enticed other out-of-towners to set up shop. At the rambling Black Walnut Bed & Breakfast, innkeepers Peter and Lori White (who used to own bakeries in Palm Beach and Martha's Vineyard) serve lavish three-course breakfasts that might include apple crisp or raisin scones with clotted cream. After buying the 110-year-old building, the Whites undertook a top-down renovation—rooms now have fireplaces, marble baths, and 600-thread-count sheets.

Still, Asheville's real draw is access to the outdoors. The mountains seem to peek out from behind buildings in every corner of town. Even George Vanderbilt felt the pull: in 1895 he built his 250-room Biltmore Estate, the country's largest private residence, surrounded by 75 acres of Frederick Law Olmsted–designed gardens. Two hotels—the Inn on Biltmore, located right on the property, and the new Grand Bohemian Hotel Asheville, just steps from the gates—are your chance to spend the night, Vanderbilt-style. +

For The Guide, see page 264.

Clockwise from below: Tops Bar-B-Q; Cozy Corner's grilled Cornish game hen with Wonder Bread; Val Bradley of Cozy Corner with her granddaughter.

MEMPHIS

Barbecue joints that smoke the competition

IN THE RICH CANON OF AMERICAN REGIONAL FOOD, nothing quite compares to barbecue in Memphis. Though ribs are serious business in this town, it's the pork sandwich that cements a pit master's reputation. The flavor and texture of the meat may vary—depending on how each joint works its "fire"—but the basic composition remains the same: slow-roasted pork shoulder pulled (shredded by hand) or chopped (with a heavy cleaver) and piled onto a burger-like bun, then spread with a layer of tangy slaw (there may or may not be a squirt of sauce).

A Tennessee chain that's been around since 1952, Tops Bar-B-Q makes a fine introduction to Memphis eats. The

Bartender Harry Sinclair at Charlie Vergos' Rendezvous.

hickory-flavored chopped sandwich combo with mustardy slaw and beans will fortify you while you plan the rest of your odyssey. At Cozy Corner, the grilled rib tips get their share of attention, but the barbecued Cornish game hen—rich and moist all the way through—rules the roost. And if you're game to try barbecue spaghetti, Cozy's is the place to do it: sweet, tangy barbecue sauce–coated noodles actually make sense after you've spent a few days eating in Memphis.

At Neely's Bar-B-Que, don't miss the succulent pulled-pork platter, served with amazingly rich beans—sweet and thick with threads of caramelized meat. The dark wood paneling and oversize booths make the space seem like a roadhouse tavern, till the aroma sets you straight. Finally, in an alleyway basement in the business district, you'll find Charlie Vergos' Rendezvous and its famous 'Vous-style ribs (dusted with spices, including bay leaf and oregano). Bonus: a maze of dining rooms packed with fascinating bric-a-brac and Memphis paraphernalia. +

For The Guide, see page 264.

PALM BEACH

Soaking up the old-school glamour

Staffer Brady Goodman at Dolce Antiques, above. Opposite: The oceanside pool at the Breakers Palm Beach.

FROM THE 1950'S TO THE 80'S, society portrait photographer Slim Aarons focused his lens on what he described as "attractive people doing attractive things in attractive places." Campy and amusing, these images helped give rise to what can only be described as the Palm Beach Slim Aarons fantasy. But the town of Palm Beach itself—lush, hospitable, and flamboyantly attired—far exceeds its somewhat arch reputation.

The Imperial Suite at the Breakers Palm Beach.

First up: a glimpse at the lavish residences of the locals, best accomplished with a stroll along the Intracoastal Waterway (nicknamed the Trail of Conspicuous Consumption). The 1960's Regency pads, with their black glazed driveways and drive-through hedges, are among the area's indigenous delights. Stylish denizens invariably dump their cast-off furniture and tchotchkes at the South Dixie Highway vintage shops in West Palm Beach; since many of them decorated their retirement pads during the 60's and 70's, the wares—Lucite end tables, Paul Evans chairs—are some of the most collectible in the world. The short list of great secondhand stores includes Shi & Erhard, Dolce Antiques, and Shi Shi Gallery.

Vintage shopping aside, an absence of chaos is Palm Beach's most valuable asset. The lack of anything much to do, combined with the natural beauty of the surroundings, forces even the most wound-up soul to surrender to the restorative

Clockwise from top left: The dining room at Bistro Chez Jean-Pierre; antiques mecca Shi & Erhard; the Intracoastal Waterway trail.

power of reading, walking on the beach, lounging poolside at the Breakers, napping, and eating. This change-resistant town has avoided any culinary innovation of the past several decades; it is not the place to come for foams, test tubes, or chocolate martinis. Instead you'll find an emphasis on simple, 1950's digestible fare—yellowtail snapper for two at La Sirena; vegetable soup at Bistro Chez Jean-Pierre; banana cream pie at Palm Beach Grill. Sedate? Yes. Sleepy? Perhaps. But in Palm Beach, that's a good thing. +

For The Guide, see page 264.

NEW ORLEANS

Serving up the Crescent City's best bites

NOTHING, BUT NOTHING, HAS THE POWER to spoil New Orleans's appetite. The people of this city love to eat, and they eat it all—from simply fried oysters and perfectly dressed po' boys to nouveau spins on Cajun classics. On the edge of the Central Business District, regulars and tourists line up for breakfast at Mother's, where dishes such as grits and debris (roast-beef edges in gravy) or red-bean omelets with baked ham and biscuits are delivered to your Formica-topped table by old-time waitresses who may well call you darlin'. In the picturesque residential neighborhood of Bywater, mellow Coffea Café doubles as a

Cochon's rabbit and dumplings, below. Left: Cochon chefs and co-owners Stephen Stryjewski (far left) and Donald Link. Opposite: August restaurant.

gallery space for Big Easy artists. Try their café au lait (equal parts chicory coffee and steamed milk), sweet potato pancakes, or the savory "huevos crepe," filled with eggs and black beans and served with a side of Southern hospitality: a half-dozen bottles of hot sauce. Don't leave the neighborhood without swinging by corner restaurant Elizabeth's for lacquered praline bacon, baked in brown sugar with crumbled pecans.

Midday, the best po' boy in town can be found at the Parkway Bakery & Tavern. Whether you go for the gravy-laden roast beef or the golden fried shrimp, the basic anatomy is always the same: "dressed" (lettuce, tomato, mayonnaise, and pickles) on New Orleans–style French bread from the celebrated Leidenheimer Bakery. For a new spin, try the oyster loaf—fried oysters layered between two slices of buttery white bread—at Casamento's, a Garden District institution that's only open during the cooler "r" months (September, October, and so on).

When night falls, one of the best tables in town can be found at August, in a four-story French-Creole warehouse. Chef John Besh is a longtime champion of artisanal producers and area farmers—which means you might find a sugar-and-spice duckling served with Anson Mills heirloom Carolina corn grits. Down the street at Cochon, Donald Link and Stephen Stryjewski turn out splendid boudin, andouille, and smoked bacon. Order absolutely anything: from the wood-fired oyster roast to catfish court bouillon. And whatever you do, don't forget to try the fresh chunk-pineapple and cornmeal upside-down cake, slightly sticky with caramel sauce. The last bite—like this town itself—will leave you wanting more. +

For The Guide, see page 264.

Lake Superior's Pictured Rocks, near Munising, left. Below: A server at the Harbor Haus. Opposite: Main Street in Marquette, with a view of the lake.

THE UPPER PENINSULA

Tracing the vestiges of Americana

SOME PLACES SIMPLY RESONATE with a quirky, nearly forgotten history. Like Alaska, Appalachia, and Amish country, Michigan's Upper Peninsula is an out-of-the-way, out-of-the-past American preserve best discovered behind the wheel.

Start on the southern shore of Lake Superior in Munising, the departure point for three-hour boat tours along the Pictured Rocks, a 15-mile stretch of sandstone cliffs and caverns. Route 28 runs westward from here along the shoreline to Au Train, where Red Barn Antiques lies a few miles off the main road. Its tables are filled with agate, hematite, and crystalline formations of rosy metal—a preview of the so-called Copper Country's geological treasures. West of Au Train is Lakenenland, a roadside sculpture park where visionary welder Tom Lakenen has turned industrial scrap into whimsical large-scale monuments.

A word to the wise: The U.P. is not one of those places where hotels come with fancy linens or 24-hour room service. In these parts, lodges, cabins, and motels have mounted deer heads and a nonironic use of knotty pine. The six-floor Landmark Inn, overlooking Lake Superior in Marquette, is a lovely exception; built in the grand style of the 1930's, the property has played host to visitors as varied as Amelia Earhart and Maya Angelou.

In Baraga, stop by the Drive-In, a classic burger joint where a teenage waitress will clip a tray to your car window and take your order. Follow the Portage River to the towns of Houghton and Hancock, where you can prowl the grounds of the Quincy Mine and stop at Amy J's Pasty for the ultimate U.P. specialty: traditional Cornish ground-meat-and-potato pies.

From the highway, Calumet rises up seemingly out of nowhere, a landscape of pitched roofs and church spires. Ghosts of the region's history abound: a 1,720-pound specimen of native copper is planted in the ground outside the Harbor Haus, where waitresses in dirndls serve grilled Lake Superior trout. Much like the Upper Peninsula itself, the restaurant exists on the remnants of the past. Watching the sun set on the great lake with the jagged cliffs beyond, it's easy to see how much—and how little—the world has changed. +

For The Guide, see page 265.

Leo's Grill & Malt Shop, on Main Street, below. Right: Taking home a secondhand treasure. Opposite: The dining room at the Lowell Inn.

STILLWATER

Antiquing in the heartland

HUGGING THE LIMESTONE BANKS of the St. Croix River, this 19th-century lumber boomtown has long lured Twin City weekenders with its quaint nostalgic charm. Many of them ended up staying—opening wine bars, turning Victorian mansions into inns, and giving the tight-knit community a cosmopolitan air.

Staples Mill Antiques, a co-op of 35 dealers housed in a 50-year-old stone sawmill, is stocked with everything from stacks of *Life* magazines to cases of Depression glass and costume jewelry. Midtown Antique Mall hosts 90 dealers in a three-story structure; the top level is a giant furniture gallery crammed with Mission, Colonial, Deco, and other pre-1950's styles. Farther up Main Street at Rose Mille, vintage fabrics, buttons, and trims are sold next to retro mirrors, light fixtures, and women's clothing. Stillwater is also a mecca for bibliophiles: at St. Croix Antiquarian Booksellers, owner Gary Goodman dispenses an encyclopedic knowledge of his own 40,000-volume rare and out-of-print book collection.

Find sustenance at the mom-and-pop Leo's Grill & Malt Shop, which serves the town's best burgers, fries, and malteds. Then bed down at the Rivertown Inn, a meticulously restored Victorian with period furnishings and salvaged stained-glass windows. Or for even more bygone ambience, check in at the Lowell Inn—which has giant crystal chandeliers, wall murals, and a parlor made for sitting and sipping an old-fashioned. +

For The Guide, see page 265.

ASPEN

High-altitude hot spot

ALMOST EVERYONE HAS AN OPINION OF ASPEN—a town where Hunter S. Thompson once ran for sheriff, and world conferences draw hordes of VIP's and even more plainclothes security men. Rugged and pristine, sophisticated and simple, Aspen is nothing if not full of contrasts. But a few things are for certain: the winter air is crisp and invigorating, and the scenery in all directions is simply staggering.

The star-studded side of town is on view at the Aspen Meadows Resort and its on-site Aspen Institute, where Bill Clinton, the Dalai Lama, and Jordan's Queen Noor have attended public panels. Restaurants and nightlife are equally high-profile. At Montagna, inside the classic ski-in, ski-out hotel the Little Nell, 35-year-old chef Ryan Hardy sources produce and meat from his own organic farm. Tapas-style plates like Kobe meatballs and Boursin-cheese mashers are the specialties at the sleek lounge Social—owned by a team that includes Gunnar Sachs, son of original international playboy Gunter

Clockwise from above: The whirlpool at Aspen Meadows Resort; on the slopes; restaurateurs Tommy Tolleson (far left), Denise Walters, and Gunnar Sachs at Elevation. Opposite: Aspen at dusk.

Sachs. In the same building, long-standing favorite Elevation serves *açai* martinis so delicious that the bartender hides the Brazilian nectar to keep the staff from sneaking off with it.

But above all, Aspen is an outdoor fantasyland, offering everything from ice climbing and ice fishing to snowmobiling and cross-country skiing. In addition to Aspen Mountain (or Ajax, as the locals call it), there's Snowmass, where a colossal $1 billion base development is under way. Everywhere you go, you'll hear people talk about "the Bowl"—the legendary Highland Bowl, on Aspen Highlands mountain, a free 10-minute shuttle ride from town. Getting to the summit involves a Sno-Cat ride and a precipitous hike (with skis strapped to your back) up to a 12,392-foot peak. All is forgiven, however, once you're plowing knee-deep through champagne powder—the reason so much hype about Aspen ever existed in the first place. +

For The Guide, see page 265.

CENTRAL NEW MEXICO

High-desert drive with quirky finds

THE NORTHERN PART OF NEW MEXICO is what most travelers know, but its midsection is a true surprise: sprawling, craggy desert full of eccentric charm and no shortage of superlatives. Where else in the span of 500 miles can you find the country's oldest continually inhabited Indian pueblo; an internationally acclaimed art installation; the largest collection of radio telescopes in the world; and a town devoted entirely to pies?

The journey begins an hour south of Santa Fe in the town of Bernalillo, which lies in the shadow of the 10,378-foot Sandia Crest. Heading west on Interstate 40, the urban sprawl of Albuquerque gives way to wide, lonely landscapes en route to Acoma Pueblo, an 860-year-old, still-inhabited "sky city" atop a 370-foot-high sandstone mesa. You can buy crafts and jewelry from Acoma artisans, shop for hand-coiled local pottery, and dine at the Yaaka Café on traditional specialties like beef pozole and lamb stew.

The blink-and-you'll-miss-it outpost of Quemado is an unlikely place to find cutting-edge land art. But Dia Art Foundation's *The Lightning Field* is both impressive and provocative—a meditation on unexpected symmetry amid natural chaos. In 1977, sculptor Walter de Maria stuck more than 400 stainless-steel poles in a stark desert basin (the name comes from the poles' propensity to attract electrical strikes during summer storms). The site can accommodate only six visitors at a time; you check in at the Dia office in Quemado, and are taken to stay overnight in a rustic log cabin with

Above, from left: In the town of Magdalena; owner Kathy Knapp of Pie-O-Neer, in Pie Town.
Opposite: Bird watching at Bosque del Apache National Wildlife Refuge.

three bedrooms, a fridge stocked with enchiladas, and a porch that opens right onto the exhibit. Even the caretaker, a reticent and rangy cowboy straight out of *No Country for Old Men*, seems like part of the installation.

From Quemado, Highway 160 leads east to tiny Pie Town, named after a homegrown apple-pie business in the 1920's. The town still lives up to its reputation, thanks to the Daily Pie Café and the newer Pie-O-Neer. It's 36 miles farther to the Very Large Array, the Southwest's most surreal roadside attraction— a collection of 27 giant satellite dishes used by astronomers to study radio waves emitted by stars and planets. Next stop is Magdalena, a pioneer settlement and artists' colony; from there, continue on to the city of Socorro, a 16th-century trading post. End at the nearby Bosque del Apache National Wildlife Refuge, a lush habitat for pelicans and sandhill cranes. +

For The Guide, see page 265.

Saguaro National Park, just outside Tucson.

TUCSON

Dude ranches and destination dining

ALL HAIL THE SAGUARO CACTUS—a plant that can weigh up to eight tons and live more than 150 years, thriving in the harsh light of the Sonoran Desert. It's the de facto icon of southern Arizona, a parched and prickly region of acacia, mesquite, and cacti. But don't think of this as your average desert: there are mountains (sometimes even snow), as well as a surprisingly vibrant restaurant scene.

North of Tucson, the Santa Catalina range is where locals head for a cool break from the blazing summer heat. Take the winding, scenic highway to the top of 9,157-foot Mount Lemmon and the resort village of Summerhaven, where the Mt. Lemmon General Store sells sinful slabs of homemade fudge (especially irresistible: the cookie-dough variety). Just outside Tucson, Saguaro National Park provides the ultimate overview of this desert ecosystem—green paloverde, purple cacti, and fuzzy teddy-bear cholla. Indulge your city-slicker fantasies at Tanque Verde Ranch, where a horse comes with your vacation and wranglers lead sunset rides into the wilderness. In the mood for Old Hollywood glamour? The Arizona Inn has croquet on the lawn and a starlet-worthy pool.

A sampling of Tucson's best restaurants proves there's more to Southwestern cuisine than the three C's (chile, corn, and cilantro). Whether it's sausage and biscuits or "eggs & gunpowder," breakfast at the Hotel Congress's Cup Café is funky and fun. Behind the RumRunner wine shop lies the Dish, a bistro with a well-priced midweek dinner special: a bowl of mussels and a glass of wine for $11.50. Hit Café Poca Cosa for innovative updates on regional favorites—look for recurring items like *pollo en pipián* or the popular tamale pie. And at Janos, James Beard Award winner Janos Wilder peppers his dishes with native ingredients like cholla buds, mesquite flour, and saguaro blossoms. +

For The Guide, see page 266.

Cupcakes at Twentyfive Main, a café in St. George, left.
Bottom left: The Brigham Young House, one of St. George's
Mormon sites. Below: Dining at Red Mountain Resort & Spa.

UTAH AND NEVADA

Where the scenery is the star

"WELCOME TO THE GREATEST EARTH ON SHOW," declares one highway sign. Those words couldn't be truer about this drive from Las Vegas through Nevada and Utah—where the sky is vast, the landscape is alive, the cowboy hats are big, and the pickup trucks come caked and splattered with red dirt. This is the real American Southwest, with a wildness and emptiness that allows you a taste of frontier life.

Twenty miles outside of Las Vegas, the I-15 freeway traffic starts to peter out, and a realization sets in: this is 100 percent desert. Stop for a hike through Nevada's Valley of Fire State Park, where red sandstone forms odd geological structures, such as beehive- and piano-shaped stones.

The drive north passes through Joshua tree–strewn desert and canyons, ending at the 19th-century Mormon settlement of St. George. East of St. George is Springdale, whose main drag is lined with motels and adventure outfitters. The draw here is nature—you're at the entrance of Zion National Park. The village-like Flanigan's Inn is a popular overnight option;

or for easy access to the park's trails, bunk in a cabin at Zion Lodge, the only accommodation—other than campsites—inside the park itself.

Northwest of St. George lies Silver Reef, a ghost town with an 1879 Wells Fargo bank and the detour-worthy Cosmopolitan Restaurant. West of St. George, Red Mountain Resort & Spa melds pampering with fitness—an adventure concierge helps guests take full advantage of the surroundings. In these parts, sunsets are an event, with the mesas and cliffs morphing from maroon and orange into green, purple, and black. There's nothing to do but drop your jaw. ✦

For The Guide, see page 266.

IDAHO

A bracing mix of
outdoor adventures

TWO CENTURIES AGO, ON A TREK through America's uncharted interior, Lewis and Clark nearly met their match. They were ready for almost anything—woolly mammoths, cannibals, magma-spewing volcanoes—but it was a Rocky Mountain snowstorm that almost did them in. Eventually they had to start shooting their horses for food. "I have been wet and as cold in every part as I ever was in my life," William Clark wrote of the experience.

Idaho has kept a low profile ever since, with a public image that's a vague and slightly forbidding amalgam of rugged terrain and climactic extremes. Its minimal visibility has allowed the state to remain an untamed American

Idaho Rocky Mountain Ranch, in the Sawtooth Range south of Stanley. Opposite: Horseback riding at Wapiti Meadow Ranch.

A Wapiti Meadow Ranch guide prepares to fish, above left. Right: Wapiti's main lodge.

wilderness. But with the right guide, these expanses become an arena for adventure: plunging white water, seemingly impassable Rocky Mountain peaks, and trout-filled rivers.

At Idaho Rocky Mountain Ranch, the Sawtooth Range looms in the distance, and log cabins come with rustic stone fireplaces and pine furniture. Nine miles down the road is Stanley (population 70), the summer base for multiple adventure outfitters. The plum assignment is rafting the Middle Fork of the Salmon River— 100 miles of Class III and IV white water running through the largest contiguous designated-wilderness area in the Lower 48.

In nearly unpopulated Johnson Creek valley, Wapiti Meadow Ranch

first opened its doors to guests 80 years ago; it's nearly as remote now as it was back then. The pleasures of life in the mountains—hunting, fishing, riding, hiking—haven't changed much, either. Climb into the hills to find a bluff overlooking the entire valley, with its broad, limpid river under an epic mountain sky.

If Idaho were a religion, trout fishing would be its sacrament. The most storied streams are the Henry's Fork and the South Fork of the Snake River, both in eastern Idaho. A hideaway built by Mark Rockefeller, South Fork Lodge, is located right next to one of the best stretches of trout water in the state. The lazy flow of the Snake is peaceful compared with the Middle Fork of the Salmon; you can ease your boat into the current and drift through an otherwise inaccessible canyon landscape, where eroded layers of lava stand at the top of steep green slopes like battlements. "There are four or five thousand trout per mile in this river," says South Fork Lodge guide Darren Puetz. "I've never had anyone not catch a fish." If only Lewis and Clark had been so lucky. +

For The Guide, see page 266.

Takeoff in Stanley. Clockwise from below: Rafting guide Lanelle Fischer on the Middle Fork of the Salmon; fly-fishing in Wapiti Meadow Ranch's Johnson Creek; wilderness guide David Fields.

Shopping for jewelry at Souvenir, below.
Right, from top: Antique furnishings at
Hitchcock; the goods at Velouria.

SEATTLE

Shopping with the city's
creative counterculture

FOR A QUICK PRIMER ON SEATTLE'S FLOURISHING INDIE SCENE, head to
Madrona—a neighborhood on the edge of Lake Washington
where historic buildings make for a small-town feel. But not
everything here is old-fashioned: talented young designers are
setting up shop behind the traditional brick facades, infusing
the area with a fresh sensibility. One of the most exciting
newcomers is Lee Rhodes, whose handblown votives are on
display at Glassybaby, a boutique-slash-studio where visitors
can watch the elegant vessels being made. On Madrona's main
shopping street, Hitchcock sells semiprecious jewelry, vintage
furnishings and housewares, and Midcentury pieces of art.

To the northwest, Ballard is known for its Scandinavian
flavor and fishing-village past, but a crop of openings is putting
this neighborhood on trendsetters' maps. The curiosity shop
Souvenir is the brainchild of artist Curtis Steiner, whose
1,000 Blocks project is in the Seattle Art Museum's permanent
collection. At Velouria, proprietor Tes
de Luna deals in colorful frocks, silk-
screened tops, hand-sewn bags, and
letterpress stationery. Most labels hail
from the Northwest; the best include
Portland-based Elizabeth Dye, a line
of 60's-inspired dresses, and de Luna's
own brand, the flirty Zuzupop. A few
streets away, Pulp Lab is more like a
gallery than a retail outlet—owner
Kate Pawlicki commissions limited-
edition items like T-shirts and art
prints from a group of witty brands
and hosts exhibitions to introduce
them to the public. +

For The Guide, see page 266.

NAPA VALLEY

Romance amid the vines

Strolling by the main pool at Auberge du Soleil.

TIME SEEMS TO STAND STILL in the Napa Valley, where a pitch-perfect mix of wineries, restaurants, and hotels adds up to the ultimate wine lover's escape. But there's always something else to discover. The big news in the valley is the Bardessono, a 62-room property in the town of Yountville that aims to be the greenest luxury hotel in the country. Solar panels and salvaged materials provide environmental cred; in-room massage tables, outdoor showers, and rooftop cabanas give it the pampering edge. Also in Yountville is Bottega Napa Valley, the latest restaurant from celebrity chef Michael Chiarello, where the seasonal Italian menu features dishes such as pumpkin risotto and goat's milk–braised lamb shank. Just a half-hour drive north, in Angwin, Napa's most buzzed-about tasting room is the solar-powered steel-and-wood space at Cade Winery, which produces a memorable Howell Mountain Cabernet.

Of course, the classics are still a draw: Angèle, a wood-beamed bistro on the Napa River, and Round Pond Estate, known for its olive oils as well as its wines. Romantic retreats include the Provençal-inspired Auberge du Soleil (whose in-room fireplaces and private hot tubs are ideal for couples) and the Poetry Inn, with views of the hillside from the king-size beds. +

For The Guide, see page 267.

LOS ANGELES

Embracing a new authenticity

IN LOS ANGELES, WHICH HAS LONG CLUNG TO THE NOTION of unending youth, a quiet, organic movement has emerged from finding value in the old. It's not about preservation or conservation per se. It's about stewardship—of buildings and neighborhoods that carry history, and of passed-down skills. Quite simply, L.A. has awakened to its past: its stories, its people, its places.

In her factory in Downtown's Fashion District, designer Christina Kim transforms fashion-industry fabric scraps into luscious, labor-intensive clothes, seen on Nicole Kidman

Joyriding in a 1958 Corvette. Opposite: The Eastern Columbia Building, a Deco gem in L.A.'s Downtown.

Fashion designer Christina Kim at dosa818, her downtown atelier.

and Jennifer Aniston. Her ethereal aesthetic carries over to dosa818, a retail space on the 12th floor of the Wurlitzer Building on Broadway. The 7,000-square-foot loft could easily be mistaken for a Zendo, were it not for the art installations and racks of gossamer dresses.

Nightlife impresario and preservationist Andrew Meieran transformed an abandoned power plant into the Edison, one of downtown's hottest clubs—where a gigantic cast-iron generator makes you feel like a stowaway in the engine room of a Jules Verne submarine. A mile away, the vaudeville-era Orpheum Theatre attracts performers like Lyle Lovett and Alanis Morissette, and the restored Mayan Theater hosts the cult spectacle *Lucha Vavoom*, a chaotic mingling of burlesque dancers, masked Mexican wrestlers, and lowrider cars. On Sunset Boulevard in Hollywood, Amoeba Music is a monument to vinyl, an emblem of the once-indomitable record industry as it pretzels into an iTunes world. Shopping here is as much about touch and sight as about hearing—placing your fingers on record albums, responding viscerally to seductive cover art.

If L.A. is coming into its own, it's because it is learning to embrace the contradictions that define any great city. Downtown's Eastern Columbia Building, a turquoise Deco

Glimpses of L.A.'s creative scene, clockwise from top left: Staffers at Amoeba Music; puppets at the Bob Baker Marionette Theater; author Dave Eggers's Echo Park Time Travel Mart; artist Amy Bessone in her studio.

jewel converted to condominium lofts, is a far cry from neighboring South Park, a cluster of glittering skyscrapers. And on Broadway, Clifton's Brookdale Cafeteria—opened in 1935 as a haven from the Great Depression—is a far cry from just about everything else. Picture a dining hall patterned after a hunting lodge as designed by Mad King Ludwig of Bavaria. A 20-foot waterfall washes through the center of the dining room, and columns disguised as redwoods appear to poke through the ceiling. This is a bona-fide (if slightly batty) dining institution. "We are a landmark," says restaurant manager Robert Clinton, grandson of founder Clifford Clinton. "We don't need a plaque on the door to say so." Leave it to the city of eternal youth to constantly flout the old clichés. +

For The Guide, see page 267.

WAIKIKI

Where paradise is still paradise

LIKE THE MARQUESAS ISLANDERS said to have paddled here an aeon ago in colossal canoes, travelers come to Waikiki to find themselves. Real aloha, however, is not always easy to uncover. Waikiki's public face is the oceanfront proscenium of grand tourist hotels, a kind of mid-Pacific version of Potemkin Village. But the new Waikiki Beach Walk summons up something of the aura of the resort in bygone days, when the *Lurline* carried well-heeled San Franciscans and Angelenos to a manicured Pacific playground—where greeters hung leis around visitors' necks upon arrival, with an aloha that was not yet part of the script.

The modern-day skyline of Waikiki Beach.

Paddle-surfing the waters, below.
Right: The lobby of the Kahala Hotel.

For years, you had to pass through a weather-beaten strip of motels and fast-food restaurants to reach the Halekulani, a fabled hotel that stood in chastely monied anonymity amid the urban muddle. After the Waikiki Beach Walk transformed the hotel's surroundings with its update on Hawaiiana—meandering paths lined with fan palms and lit with tiki torches—the Halekulani was similarly refreshed. Every night at its open-air beachfront bar and restaurant, shaded by an ancient kiawe, a trio plays bass and slack-key guitar and sings Hawaiian tunes that have been performed here for decades.

One result of Hawaii's century of cultural blending is the parade of local beauties visible any day along Kalakaua Avenue. Don a pair of flip-flops and fall into the flow, in no particular direction; you might end up at Diamond Head, or Kapiolani Park, or the undulating walkways of the Honolulu Zoo. Spend a day swimming off the reef-protected beach at the Kahala Hotel, a 1964 colossus where one's sense of remove is absolute. In its former incarnation as a Hilton, when it was known as Kahollywood, Richard Burton and Liz Taylor would hide out from the paparazzi in a private cabana. Present-day visitors still come to hide out—if only from their cell phones. +

For The Guide, see page 267.

ALASKA

Entering the 49th state of mind

Salmon at Redoubt Bay Lodge, left.
Below: Mount McKinley and Denali
National Park, as seen from a plane.
Opposite: Wilderness guide Amy Smith
at Redoubt Bay Lodge.

OVERSIZE MOUNTAINS, remote fly-in lodges, spectacular wildlife—not to mention glaciers, seaplanes, and an endless supply of fresh salmon. They're all part of the classic Alaskan summer itinerary, an intense immersion in the alternate universe that is America's 49th state.

Board a floatplane in Anchorage, and fly to Redoubt Bay Lodge, set on a 170,000-acre state-managed preserve that's thick with bears (thanks in part to massive runs of salmon). Kirsten Dixon, who owns the property with her husband, Carl, takes wilderness cooking to a whole new level with an incredible bounty of fresh ingredients—from halibut to berries and fiddlehead ferns, which Dixon regularly forages herself. Hire a guide and paddle across the lake to Wolverine Cove, one of the few places in the world where brown and black bears interact regularly.

To get to Denali National Park, the crown jewel of Alaskan tourism, you have to face a cruel reality of Alaskan travel: logistics. (In a huge state with few roads, getting from A to B requires perseverance.) From Anchorage, the Alaska Railroad makes a seven-hour trip to the entrance of the park, passing narrow gorges, swift-rushing streams, and steep valleys framed by

A few of the cabins at Redoubt Bay, left.
Below: The dining room at Redoubt Bay Lodge.

craggy mountains. The park itself is larger than Massachusetts, with only a single, unpaved road; no private cars are allowed, so if you're headed to Camp Denali, prepare for an additional seven hours on a bus. ("Seven hours on a bus": possibly the five most heartbreaking words in the English language.) Pass the time by keeping an eye out for grizzly bears, Dall sheep, caribou, and wolves, as well as views of Mount McKinley, the tallest mountain in North America. The 18 cabins at Camp Denali—close enough to the main lodge for comfort, far enough for privacy—are popular with naturalists and researchers, who come for the resort's summer lecture series (topics range from global warming to the aurora borealis). Bush flying is another quintessential Denali experience: you can buzz around the mountain and, weather permitting, land on one of the glaciers that flow down its flanks.

Forty miles southeast of Anchorage, the town of Girdwood is the Alaskan version of Palm Springs. It's also home to the Alyeska Resort, the only hotel in the state to which the word *luxurious* can plausibly be applied. A gondola runs from the hotel to the 2,500-foot-high ski mountain, as well as the Seven Glaciers restaurant, a formal dining room with views of the lush valley and the fjordlike Turnagain Arm. In this refined setting, it's easy to feel like you're floating in a bubble, ensconced once again in the protective embrace of civilization. But elsewhere in Alaska, the truth is self-evident: wilderness is still a formidable force. ✦

For The Guide, see page 267.

MONTREAL

A Francophile's winter wonderland

TAKE PARIS, STIR IN SOME MAPLE LEAVES, drop the temperature 10, 20—or 30—degrees, and you've got Montreal: one of the world's largest French-speaking cities, complete with its own Notre Dame and Latin Quarter, not to mention patisseries galore. Stroll the cobblestoned streets of Vieux-Montréal and set off by horse-drawn sleigh through the 500 acres of Parc du Mont-Royal, the hill for which the city was named. The chill in the air is the perfect excuse for frequent pastry and *chocolat chaud* pit stops—locals swear by the *palmiers* from Olive et Gourmando and the croissants and quiche across the street at the restaurant Marché de la Villette.

Time your trip to coincide with the Fête des Neiges, Montreal's annual winter festival, which camps in Parc Jean-Drapeau on Île Sainte Hélène for three weekends of ice sculpting, snow tubing, and dogsledding. Need to thaw out? Get lost underground—there's a subterreanean world with 21 miles of walkways that connect metro stations, shops, and hockey arenas. For dinner in this exceptional food city, order *steak frites* (served with a jar of cornichons) or a *croque monsieur* at L'Express. Or dive into a menu of 60 *fromages* at Chez Gautier, in the Latin Quarter. Bed down in Vieux-Montréal's 31-room Auberge Bonaparte, whose balconies overlook the basilica of Notre Dame—home to a 7,000-pipe organ, and maybe even a hunchback. ✛

For The Guide, see page 268.

Marché de la Villette, above. Right: The historic Marché Bonsecours, which houses galleries, shops, and restaurants, near Notre Dame.

NIAGARA FALLS

Taking in the liquid assets

MOST VISITORS TO NIAGARA FALLS HEAD STRAIGHT TO CANADA—and for good reason. This is, in fact, not one waterfall but three, each of them crashing into the lower Niagara River. And although both the American and the Bridal Veil falls are situated stateside, Canada's single cascade, the Horseshoe, is larger than the other two combined—and has a riverbank with picture-perfect vantage points to see it all.

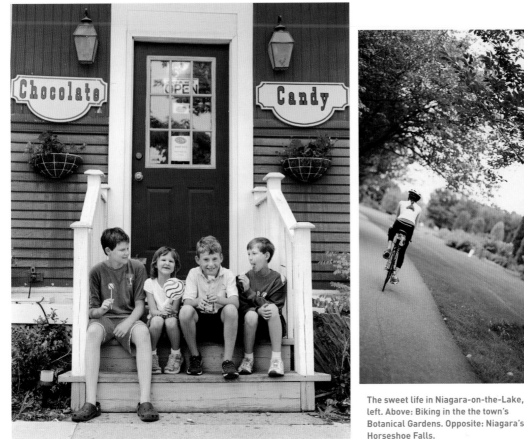

The sweet life in Niagara-on-the-Lake, left. Above: Biking in the the town's Botanical Gardens. Opposite: Niagara's Horseshoe Falls.

At the Skylon Tower, windowed elevators nicknamed "yellow bugs" depart from the lobby and ascend 775 feet above the river to an observation deck and rotating restaurant overlooking the twinkling lights of Ontario. If you can't get enough, book a room with floor-to-ceiling windows at Sheraton on the Falls—a glassy high-rise that peers down on the spectacle, which is illuminated by colored spotlights every day at dusk. On weekends from mid-May to mid-October, a fireworks display adds to the sensory overload.

A wholly different kind of liquid pursuit is on hand 15 miles north in the town of Niagara-on-the-Lake, where the Hillebrand Winery makes a fine place to sample the region's ice wine (minors can guzzle sparkling grape juice). Settle in at the Harbour House Hotel, a shingle-style inn with a maritime feel. A bike ride to the former British stronghold of Fort George takes you past the pink roses and cherry trees of the Botanical Gardens; you can follow the riverside Niagara Garden Trail all the way to Victoria Park, the closest spot on the Canadian side to Horseshoe Falls. Daredevils can opt for the Whirlpool Jet ride— a turbo-powered boat that takes off at 50 miles an hour, heading for Class V rapids, and does a 360-degree "wheelie" in 12-foot waves. (Want even more thrills? Sit in the section dubbed "OH.MY.GOD.") Your immersion is complete. +

For The Guide, see page 268.

A suite at Jade
Mountain resort,
in St. Lucia.

THE CARIBBEAN

San Juan

A flashy restaurant scene

The lobby at La Concha hotel, above. Opposite: Condado Beach, backed by new development.

"PEOPLE WHO THINK IT'S ALL ABOUT RICE AND BEANS will be surprised," Roberto Treviño says of San Juan's flourishing dining scene. Treviño, an *Iron Chef* veteran, chose Condado—the city's current nexus of all things fabulous—for his latest venture, the Asian-Latin restaurant Budatai. Only a 15-minute drive from Old San Juan, Condado feels like another country—where the people look like they just stepped off a catwalk, not a cruise ship. The neighborhood has had a major face-lift, not unlike some of the flawlessly manicured shoppers who frequent Ashford Avenue, Condado's answer to Rodeo Drive. Luxury condos, posh boutiques (including those of Puerto Rican designers Lisa Cappalli and Nono Maldonado), and swanky beach bars join a host of recently opened restaurants. At Ummo Argentinean Grill, the specialty is *parrillada*, a carnivore's banquet of chorizo, pork tenderloin, short ribs, sweetbreads, and blood sausage (the faint of heart can opt for the grilled vegetables). Meat is also front and center at Strip House, which serves up T-bones in a boudoir-inspired setting adorned with vintage burlesque photos at the Condado Plaza Hotel & Casino.

Meanwhile, at Budatai, Treviño's adventurous approach is evident in his dim sum—think Kurobuta pork profiteroles with salted caramel sauce and roast-duck blinis with wasabi crème fraîche. The view from the terrace provides proof of the area's boom-in-progress: the long-shuttered La Concha hotel, reopened as a tribute to tropical Modernism. Its owners spent $220 million on renovations but wisely spared the property's retro-cool shell, including the trademark concrete conch that houses Perla, a seafood restaurant. On weekend nights, the scene at the palm-lined pool is the epitome of Latin glamour—bronzed style mavens lounging on rattan furniture, cocktails in hand. +

For The Guide, see page 268.

Anguilla

Land of luxe hotels

Rendezvous Bay, as seen from a balcony at CuisinArt Resort.

THE BEAUTY OF ANGUILLA—which lies almost in the shadow of nearby St. Martin, with St. Bart's visible on clear days—is that it's relatively undeveloped, yet home to some of the Caribbean's most lavish resorts. The Mediterranean-style Malliouhana Hotel & Spa is still going strong after nearly 25 years, thanks in part to chef Michel Rostang's haute-French restaurant and a 25,000-bottle wine cellar. On the Caribbean side of the island, on scenic Rendezvous Bay (known for its stellar windsurfing beach), the CuisinArt Resort is a compound of low-slung, whitewashed villas with a decadent spa, fresh from a $10 million upgrade that tripled its size; you can indulge in a heated seashell massage, then feast on produce from the resort's hydroponic farm. For the first phase of an $80 million renovation at honeymooners' favorite Cap Juluca, interior designer Paul Duesing shopped the souks in Marrakesh and commissioned one-of-a-kind pieces from Moroccan craftsmen. The limestone-floored main house now has handmade rugs and century-old inlaid game tables, giving the space a romantic Moorish vibe. Opened in 2009: the 172-room Viceroy Anguilla, which brings Kelly Wearstler's signature Hollywood Regency style to a 35-acre beachfront property at the junction of Meads and Barnes bays. Expect this already-exclusive island to reach an even more dizzying level of chic. **+**

For The Guide, see page 268.

A table at the Discovery at Marigot Bay, right. Clockwise from below: The resort's Hurricane Hole bar; a vendor at the local market; the Treehouse, for private dining at the Discovery at Marigot Bay.

St. Lucia

A food-lover's idyll

A HUNDRED MILES WEST OF BARBADOS, but oceans away in tempo, St. Lucia has largely stayed blissfully below the radar. This lush volcanic island is known—if it's known at all—for rain forest–draped mountains, excellent dive sites, and a handful of small-scale resorts, like the Discovery at Marigot Bay. Now its culinary offerings are generating buzz. Those green slopes and dense forests are the source of pristine produce, including mangoes, bananas, and some of the world's finest cocoa. At Fond Doux Holiday Plantation, a working plantation and eco-resort, you can watch as cocoa pods are transformed by hand into pure chocolate. Guests can bed down in one of several 19th-century colonial cottages restored by the estate's charismatic owner, Lyton Lamontagne, who also leads informal group cooking sessions. Far more luxurious lodgings are up the road at Jade Mountain, whose vertiginous perch affords bang-on views of the Pitons, St. Lucia's iconic twin peaks. The intimate restaurant serves slow-roasted suckling pig, house-baked bread, and organic treats from the resort's own

Overlooking the Pitons at Jade Mountain, left. Below left: A bedroom at the resort. Below: The resort's infinity pool Opposite: A waterfall at the island's Diamond Botanical Gardens.

farm—tender tatsoi and mizuna lettuces, spicy watermelon radishes, fragrant herbs, even juicy tomatoes. (Where else in the Caribbean could you have a perfect salad?) The list of memorable island foods goes on: callaloo soup at the Coal Pot, homemade gelato at Rowley's Caribbean Café, cassava bread from Plas Kassav. But for an all-out party atmosphere, the place to be is at the Fish Fry each Friday night in the village of Anse la Raye. Starting at sunset, sidewalk barbecues sizzle with fresh octopus, conch, lobster, and tuna while reggae bands play and locals and tourists alike dance in the streets. +

For The Guide, see page 268.

Barbados

Retro glamour meets a modern era

ON CERTAIN FRAGRANT EVENINGS IN BARBADOS, when an overripe mango moon seems ready to burst, the island gives itself over to magical realism. An eerie lullaby—the nocturnal chirping of the whistling tree frogs—ebbs and wells like a confused concerto as the banality of daily life slips away.

Nothing in Barbados can be separated from the romance of the island's past. A stylish afternoon at the Holders Hill polo field, watching a match with some bright young English things, is akin to stepping back into the 1920's, and costs less than the price of a movie in New York. At Scarlet, a sharp little restaurant serving coq au vin and sticky toffee pudding, the bathrooms are decorated with layouts from 1960's-era British

Vogue, with Gloria Guinness adrift in a "sea of voile." Guinness was also an icon of Sandy Lane, the hotel that arrived in a storm of glamour in 1961. As with Jamaica, which has clung to the image of Noël Coward and Ian Fleming in the age of hot-tub high jinks at Hedonism VII, Barbados is in the business of myth.

But now the volume has been turned up all over the island. The Coral Reef Club launched a spa

The Crane, the oldest luxury hotel on Barbados. Opposite, clockwise from far left: Polo at Holders Hill; a Plantation Suite at Coral Reef Club; a coconut grove on the island's east coast.

Barracuda with curried lentils at Scarlet, below. Right: The clear, calm waters of the island's west coast. Opposite: A hammock with a view at the Sea-U Guest House.

overseen by Neil Howard, who worked on the Armani hotels in Dubai and Milan. The Crane, a fixture on the southeast coast since 1887, is in the midst of a multimillion-dollar expansion. A Four Seasons—the first international luxury brand-name resort on the island—is slated to open on the site of the old Paradise Beach hotel in Clearwater Bay. Little Good Harbour, where a studied informality prevails, recently took over the funky old Atlantis Hotel on the windswept east coast. And there are good bargains to be found off the track as well—like the sweet Sea-U Guest House, also on the east coast near the surfing town of Bathsheba.

The island's enduring joy is its architecture, whether the buildings are chattel houses (tiny wooden gingerbread cottages that workers would disassemble and transport from plantation to plantation) or great estates (in styles like Palladian Regency and neo-Gothic). Old houses are the true celebrities on Barbados—debated and judged as if they were Hollywood stars, denounced for either letting themselves go or, worse, having too much work done and taking a turn for the vulgar. From January through mid-April, the Barbados National Trust hosts weekly open houses; for $10, you can see everything from Oliver Messel–designed residences to the Caribbean Georgian Byde Mill house, a study in coral stone. ✦

For The Guide, see page 269.

Bequia

Still an insider's secret

Fresh coconut water at the Firefly Hotel, above left. Right: A seaside view.
Opposite: A Firefly Hotel guest room.

ITS NAME MEANS "ISLAND OF CLOUDS," but Bequia (pronounced BECK-wee) is hardly a mist-shrouded getaway—the sun shines on verdant hills, untamed beaches, and Port Elizabeth, the crescent-shaped natural harbor. A 45-minute flight from Barbados, this seven-square-mile speck of land is one of the last hidden destinations in the Caribbean. Its biggest claim to fame came from boat building, a generations-old island tradition that remains to this day (albeit on a different scale); now master craftsmen carve their vessels in miniature, with the best examples to be found at Sargeant Bros. Model Boats, in Port Elizabeth.

Rent a car and drive to the just-renovated Firefly Bequia, on a working coconut plantation that dates from the 18th century. The four-room property is full of sumptuous details, like rooms with canopied beds and double waterfall showers. It's the first in a handful of new hotels and residential developments, including Bequia Beach Hotel on Friendship Bay. There, most of the 29 rooms overlook a white-sand beach, and the terraced gardens are filled with banana, mango, and papaya trees. The spa, with its three seaside treatment rooms, is the best on the island. For lunch, order the lobster salad—and don't pass up the doughy pretzels or lime squash cocktails.

After a lazy day on the beach, head to Fernando's Hideaway, a restaurant located below chef Fernando Morgan's living quarters, which is set on stilts above Lower Bay. On the menu: the day's catch and warm apple spice cake, served up by the chef's two sisters. Meander down to the water for a view of the tranquil harbor, and marvel at how it feels to have the Caribbean to yourself. +

For The Guide, see page 269.

Well-heeled sun worshippers
in the 1980's, overlooking
Mustique's Lagoon Bay.

Mustique

Kicking back with high society

ONCE THE MOST PRIVATE OF PRIVATE ISLANDS—where you had to be known and preapproved to receive permission to fly into the mini-airport—Mustique has evolved into a postcolonial place that's open to all. There are only 100 houses on this tiny chunk of volcanic rock, smack in the middle of the island-chain nation called St. Vincent and the Grenadines. You can rent anything from a breezy two-bedroom hideaway to an extravagantly tricked-out air-conditioned dream palace. There are only two hotels: the 17-room Cotton House, reimagined in tropical-colonial style by renowned Paris-based hotelier Grace Leo-Andrieu, and the five-room Firefly Mustique. Aside from that, you'll find three restaurants, a handful of shops, nine beaches, and a fleet of golf carts (the only means of guest transportation).

Longtime denizens of the island, a mixed bag of Europeans and North and South Americans, include villa owner Mick Jagger and fashion designer Tommy Hilfiger; high-profile renters run to the likes of Beyoncé and Jennifer Lopez. But the true soul of Mustique isn't found in the residences of the rich. You'll find it instead at Basil's Bar, arguably the most famous nighttime haunt in the Caribbean— where proprietor Basil Charles, a caftan-clad perpetual party machine, serves as the island's unofficial mayor. +

For The Guide, see page 269.

Left, clockwise from top left:
The restaurant at Laluna Resort;
Laluna's pool; Grand Etang Lake;
Grenada's capital, St. George's;
a cottage at Laluna Resort.

Grenada

Caribbean without the crowds

Fragrant nutmeg trees, tropical blooms, and waterfalls that flow into the sea: for centuries, Grenada's charms remained unfamiliar to even the most well traveled. Then came the Bali-inspired Laluna Resort and the Mount Cinnamon Resort, both ushering in a new wave of sophistication. But the island's authenticity and natural beauty remain. One-sixth of Grenada—including Grand Etang, a crater lake atop an extinct volcano—is protected wilderness. Farmers still sell fresh fruit and exotic spices at the market in the colonial capital of St. George's, where the winding roads are lined with boutiques, including Tikal, which sells baskets, hand-printed batiks, and other local crafts. On Friday nights, an open-air fish fry takes over the village of Gouyave to the festive sounds of steel drums. And the beachside Aquarium restaurant makes an enticing day's end, with West Indian barbecue served beneath the stars. ✛

For The Guide, see page 269.

At the Hotel
Casa Vecchia,
in Antigua,
Guatemala.

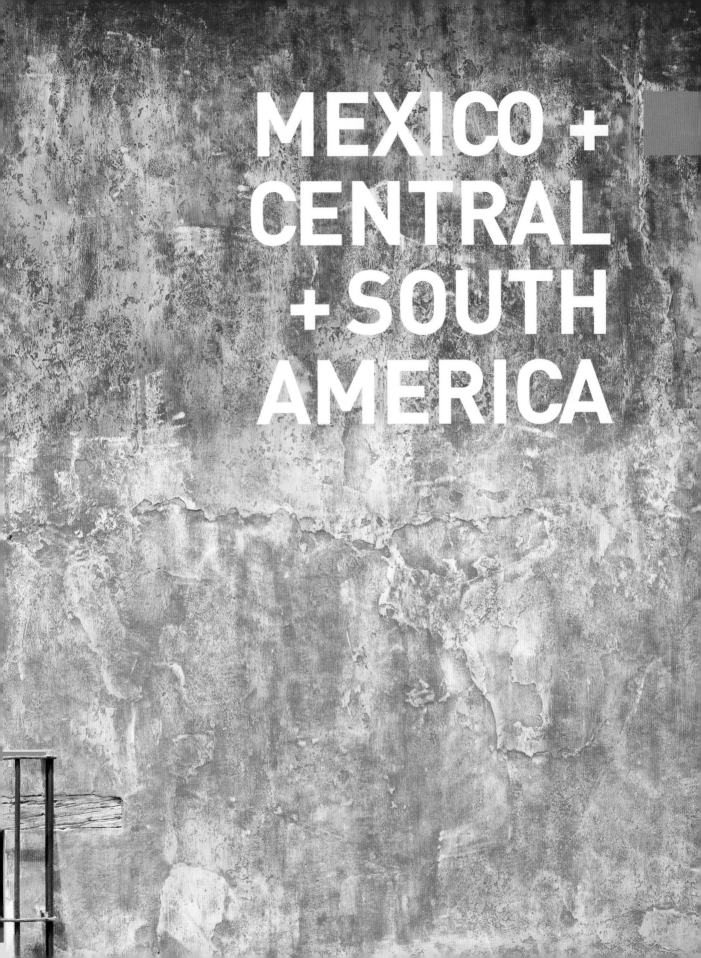

MEXICO + CENTRAL + SOUTH AMERICA

The mountains surrounding San Francisco Bay, left. Below: Harvesting clams on Baja California's Isla Coyote.

BAJA CALIFORNIA

A spectacle of sea life

THE HUNDRED OR SO VOLCANIC ISLANDS that line the coast of Baja California Sur, in the Sea of Cortes, are home to 875 fish species, a multitude of other marine animals—and 11 human beings. All it takes to explore these uncharted deserts is a catamaran, a captain, and a few days off. The largest of the islets, Isla San José, has a quiet saltwater laguna with an oyster-strewn shore—remnants of Baja's erstwhile pearl industry, the driving force behind the region's colonization in the 17th century. The lagoon makes for great snorkeling: enormous broomtail grouper weave their way through the mangrove swamp's tangle of underwater roots.

Just south of San José lies Isla San Francisco, one of the most visited in the Sea of Cortes. From the sea it looks like an archetypical desert isle—white-sand beaches defined by deep blue water. But climb the gentle slope up to the volcano's crater (like all the *islotes*, San Francisco is just the summit of an ancient submerged mountain) and the earth turns gray and pebbly, with prickly yellow bushes as the only vegetation. At these arid heights you can hear the cries of nesting eagles, and maybe even

Sea lions sunning on the island of Las Rocas.

make out the neighboring pair of islands, Isla Partida and Isla Espiritu Santo. The latter's western coastline consists of tiny coves, perfect for putting down anchor for the night and watching manta rays zigzag through the depths.

Save the best for last with a stop at Las Rocas, a tiny island where sea lions are the main inhabitants. Snorkeling just offshore provides an intimate glimpse into their active lives, as the surprisingly aerodynamic creatures zip through the water in pairs. It's a quick trip by catamaran back to the port of La Paz, but from this underwater vantage point, the hustle and bustle of the mainland feels a thousand miles away. +

For The Guide, see page 270.

MAZATLÁN

A revitalized village by the sea

Alfresco dining in Old Town, left. Below: The lobby at Casa Lucila. Opposite: The courtyard at Melville Suites.

ONCE A 19TH-CENTURY PLAYGROUND FOR EUROPEAN ARISTOCRACY, Mazatlán became a popular port for cruise ships in the 1960's—and its reputation suffered. Strip malls and chain restaurants sprouted up along the Zona Dorada, a 12-mile stretch of beach. The Neoclassical mansions, with their 16-foot ceilings and wrought-iron balconies—remnants of the destination's heyday—were abandoned and nearly forgotten.

But now Mazatlán's Centro Histórico, or Old Town, is undergoing a renaissance, with new establishments on seemingly every corner. Alfredo Gómez Rubio jump-started the trend more than 10 years ago when he transformed a dilapidated social club into Pedro y Lola, a restaurant named after Mexican actor Pedro Infante and *ranchera* singer Lola Beltrán. Soon after, artists Miguel Ruíz and his Belgian wife, Helene van der Heiden, opened Casa Etnika, a gallery where Michoacán silver necklaces are displayed next to paintings by local residents. More galleries followed, as did an overhaul of the 1874 Teatro Ángela Peralta, an Italian Renaissance–style theater with an open-air lobby and triple-tiered balconies.

Mazatlán's most memorable hotels are intimately scaled. Casa Lucila, Old Town's first seaside boutique property, was built on the site of a 1940's nightclub frequented by John Wayne and Ernest Hemingway. Overlooking Olas Altas beach, the eight rooms have custom-made mahogany doors and Italian ceramic–tiled floors. Just around the corner lies Melville Suites, a 19th-century former nunnery brimming with hand-carved armoires and Mexican antiques. The arched entryways overlook a courtyard where mariachi bands play at dusk. ✦

For The Guide, see page 270.

The 17th-century Temple of Santa María Ahuacatlán, below. Clockwise from right: Rodavento Boutique Hotel; Lake Avándaro; a *taquito dorado.*

VALLE DE BRAVO

Adventures in a pine-clad valley

ON WEEKENDS, WELL-HEELED RESIDENTS of Mexico City flee the urban sprawl for Valle de Bravo, a colonial-era getaway 90 miles southwest of the capital. The town also draws thousands of Mexican pilgrims each year to its 17th-century Temple of Santa María Ahuacatlán, whose fire-charred sculpture, Cristo Negro (Black Christ), is said to perform miracles. Valle's best place to stay, Rodavento Boutique Hotel, has 28 stylish suites in tented-roof villas and an Asian-inspired spa. Book the 90-minute Shaman Healing session for its energy-balancing massage; or seek out the weekly *temazcal* (indigenous sweat lodge) to purify body and soul.

Nowhere are the town's Mediterranean influences more evident than in its love for Italian food. At Dipao Pizza y Vino, a wood-burning oven delivers crisp thin-crust pies. For a more regional snack, head to one of the stalls on Plaza Principal and order a *taquito dorado*—filled with meat, grilled onions, sautéed squash blossoms, and *rajas* (poblano peppers). After lunch, get a bird's-eye view of Valle's mountains with a paragliding lesson from FlyMexico: you'll leap off the 7,300-foot-high Peñon de Temascaltepec, soar for a while, then touch down at the flying club's snack bar for a sandwich and *cerveza.*

Trips to nearby Lake Avándaro are festive affairs. On a three-hour nighttime sail aboard the Yate Fiesta Valle, you can join locals sipping cocktails and swiveling to live salsa music. By day, hire a guide to take you around on a J/24 racing sailboat (be sure to stop for a dip under one of the three waterfalls). Crisp air, pine forests, an idyllic lake: this is Mexico as you've never seen it. ✦

For The Guide, see page 270.

Cuernavaca at night, left. Below:
A teacher at Cuauhnáhuac's
Spanish language school.

CUERNAVACA

Learning by listening

IF STUDYING A SECOND LANGUAGE IS CALISTHENICS FOR THE BRAIN
—a mind-expanding form of self-improvement—then a total-immersion Spanish course makes for an especially worthy vacation. Just over an hour's drive from Mexico City, the small city of Cuernavaca is the country's hub for this kind of travel. At Cuauhnáhuac Intensive Spanish Language School, classes consist of no more than five people; some students stay in hotels, but most choose to board with Mexican host families selected by the school, an integral part of learning the native tongue and culture.

Extracurricular hours are spent listening to the locals. One of the best places for some friendly eavesdropping is the casual Los Arcos café on the town's *zócalo* (main plaza). A mix of ancient trees, winding walkways, and carts selling everything from tacos and juices to key chains, the *zócalo* is full of music nearly every night—spilling out from the numerous boom boxes brought by vendors. In one corner of the square, elderly couples dance to recorded tangos, solemn and romantic. Pick up whatever stray scraps of conversation you can, and eventually the magical moment will arrive—the miracle of comprehension that signals your time immersed in the Spanish language is beginning to pay off. +

For The Guide, see page 270.

BELIZE

Action-packed and affordable

YOU SAY YOU WANT D.I.Y. ADVENTURE? Belize is the place for you and your gang. From jungle to beach, the country is full of family-friendly eco options that make it easy to stick to a budget. For an after-hours walk on the wild side—complete with sleepover— there's no better place to start than the Belize Zoo. Home to more than 100 indigenous birds, mammals, and reptiles, this Belize City institution gets high marks for its conservation efforts and natural-setting enclosures. Sign your crew up for a night

At the beach in
Caye Caulker.

An array of beach activities on Caye Caulker, left. Above: On the porch of a bungalow at Caves Branch Jungle Lodge.

safari (and pet a jaguar!), then bed down in cabins overlooking a pond that attracts egrets and crocodiles.

From Belize City's busy marine terminal, a speedboat shuttles you 20 miles offshore to Caye Caulker, a narrow mangrove island with sandy streets and just a handful of cars. Book a simple cabana equipped with bunk beds and striped Mayan hammocks at De Real Macaw guesthouse, and ask the owner to recommend a guide for a snorkeling tour of the reef. Kick back in a hammock at I&I Reggae Bar—the definition of island downtime.

Sixty miles from Belize City, in the western Cayo District, Canadian adventurer Ian Anderson runs the Caves Branch Jungle Lodge in high-energy *Survivor* style: tree houses, tiki torches, and open-air showers, plus activities that range from kayaking to horseback riding and cave tubing (don a headlamp and float down underground rivers on inner tubes). For the fearless, there's the Black Hole Drop—a 280-foot-deep sinkhole with climbing ropes snaking over the edge. That's Belize: adventure, as promised. +

For The Guide, see page 270.

GUATEMALA

**Thriving culture
and a colonial past**

Outside Santa Clara, a convent in Antigua, left.
Below: Guatemala City's Palacio Nacional.
Opposite: At the market in Chichicastenango.

IN A VERDANT VALLEY RINGED BY MOUNTAINS, the city of Antigua is full of 16th-century gems. Wander the streets of this artsy colonial outpost to find the Palacio de los Capitanes Generales, with its traditional arched façade, and the Iglesia El Calvario, whose frescoed interior depicts the Stations of the Cross. Book a room at the city's best place to stay, Hotel Casa Santo Domingo, an atmospheric former convent. The food in town is as enticing as the architecture: at La Cuevita de los Urquizu, you can dine on *tamales chapines* and the traditional Guatemalan *Kak'ik* (a spicy turkey stew sopped up with tortillas).

Antigua's historical sites and the nearby capital of Guatemala City are good jumping-off points for a tour of the Mayan heartland. An hour and a half away, volcanic Lake Atitlán (which, as Aldous Huxley famously wrote, "touches the limits of the permissively picturesque—it is really too much of a good thing") has a number of villages dotting its shores. Panajachel is Atitlán's biggest town and its transportation hub—all buses arrive here, and taxi boats depart routinely throughout the day, carrying passengers and goods from one tiny port to another. In Santiago, which lies between two towering volcanoes across the lake, artisans in traditional dress sell colorful fabrics and leather goods.

But the best shopping is in nearby Chichicastenango, which hosts Central America's biggest and most famous market. On Thursdays and Sundays, indigenous people from all around the region descend on Chichi to hawk their wares—everything from intricate *huipil* blouses to carved wooden masks. On the steps of the Iglesia Santo Tomás, villagers honor their ancestors with candles, incense, and cut roses. It's a vivid display of the culture that thrived in Guatemala before Columbus ever set foot in the New World—and a stirring demonstration of resilience 500 years later. ✦

For The Guide, see page 271.

NICARAGUA

Just untamed enough

HISTORY IS ALIVE AND EVER PRESENT IN NICARAGUA. The country exudes just the right balance of comfort and exoticism; the civil war is long over, but a relatively underdeveloped, reasonably untouched authenticity remains. This is one of those Places on the Verge, discovered by cognoscenti but not yet overrun.

The most exceptional kind of ecotourism here involves volcanoes—including one dead and one very much alive. The ascent to the top of Mombacho, which last erupted about 450 years ago, is positively theme park–like: on the back of an open-air flatbed truck, occasionally at an angle of 45 degrees. On Masaya, you can drive right to the rim and stand on the volcano's lip, gazing at the thousand-foot-wide maw, the flitting parakeets that live in the crater, and

A view of Granada, one of the
oldest colonial cities in Nicaragua,

The terrace at Morgan's Rock Hacienda & Ecolodge, in San Juan del Sur, above.
Opposite: A beach on the west coast of Big Corn Island.

the clouds of sulfurous steam rising against the sky.

San Juan del Sur, just north of the Costa Rican border, could be the 21st-century equivalent of Puerto Vallarta in the early 1950's, with Morgan's Rock Hacienda & Ecolodge as its epicenter of chic. Respect for nature and authenticity meets a deeply comforting design: floors of polished dark stone, walls of rusticated volcanic rock, roofs of red tile and thatch. The view is killer—a mile-wide Pacific cove with a perfect white crescent beach.

A two-hour prop-plane flight from Managua, Big Corn Island has no casinos, no cruise ships, and no hotels with more than 20 rooms. Commercial fishing is still more important than tourism. The island's poshest place to stay is Casa Canada, which has landscaped grounds, an infinity pool, and $99-a-night bungalows instead of the rooms for $10 to $40 that are available elsewhere. Yet a sealed-off luxury compound it is not: locals gather each night for dinner, parents sipping frozen margaritas as children swing on the hanging barstools while the hotel's pet capuchin monkey scampers about.

The Platonic ideal of the Caribbean may just be found at Anastasia's on the Sea, a rustic one-room restaurant (with simple guest rooms) at the end of a pier over blue-green shallows. Cool and cozy, intimate but not claustrophobic, it has bare wooden walls with blue-and-white trim, open windows, and snorkels and flippers for rent; surrounded by nothing but sky and sea. +

For The Guide, see page 271.

THE NICOYA PENINSULA

**An uncomplicated
beach vacation**

A red mangrove tree on the beach, left. Below: Learning to surf at Playa Negra Surf School. Opposite: Hotel Playa Negra.

BEACH BUMS AND SURFERS OF ALL ABILITIES flock to this stretch of Costa Rica's Pacific Coast to unwind in easy—and relatively inexpensive—style. Base yourself at Hotel Playa Negra, a clutch of thatched-roof bungalows beside a black-sand beach with an impressive break (see for yourself in *Endless Summer II*). Days start with bountiful breakfasts at the hotel's poolside open-air rancho—platters of papaya, mango, pineapple, and banana; *gallo pinto* (rice and beans); and *tostadas francesas* (French toast). Kids can splash in the shallows or dig for hermit crabs, learn to ride waves at the on-site surf school, or join the roving band of youngsters performing cannonballs in the pool and chasing one another through the red mangrove trees. Fishing trips, horseback rides, and zipline outings in the jungle are other options, though relaxing might well be the order of the day.

At Lola's in nearby Playa Avellana, guests sit right on the sand at palm-shaded tables made from tree trunks. The Dutch-American owners serve delectable ahi-tuna sandwiches (but no pork, out of respect for their 800-pound pet pig that functions as the restaurant's namesake). Café Playa Negra, in Los Pargos, offers Peruvian cuisine and a trampoline that keeps the kids happy before and after the grilled mahi mahi. Back at the bungalows, bedtime comes with its own set of thrills—bullfrogs croaking on the doorstep and howler monkeys whooping from the trees. ✚

For The Guide, see page 271.

ATACAMA DESERT

Delving into the driest place on earth

THE NORTHERNMOST POINT OF CHILE may be 50 times more parched than California's Death Valley, but its earth is very much alive: steaming geysers, volcanoes, and canyons meld with salt lagoons, sand dunes, and oases for a heady, majestic beauty. With few clouds and virtually no light pollution, the Atacama Desert ranks among the best places in the world for stargazing. Still, one of its most thrilling sights is of the man-made variety. On the heels of luxe trailblazers like Explora Atacama and Awasi comes the 32-room Tierra Atacama Hotel & Spa—a resort crafted from unorthodox materials like oxidized iron and sandblasted glass, as well as adobe, rammed earth, and shale.

Excursions from the hotel have an epic quality. Climb to the top of 18,346-foot Láscar Volcano; walk amid the geysers at El Tatio; take a three-hour bike ride to Sejas Lagoon, a sea-green pool so saline you'll float like a buoy. Shop the market in town for crafts, and visit the 3,000-year-old abandoned village of Tulor for a greater understanding of the native culture. Back at the Tierra Atacama, head to the spa for a volcanic stone massage or a bath steeped in desert herbs. Finish with a cup of rica rica tea and a nap—a cocooning end to a day of dramatic extremes. +

For The Guide, see page 271.

High design in the desert at Tierra Atacama Hotel & Spa.

CACHI

**A far-flung
Andean escape**

HALF THE FUN OF GOING TO CACHI, a remote mountain-valley town in northwestern Argentina, is driving there from the provincial capital, Salta. The switchbacks up the Cuesta del Obispo (Bishop's Slope) afford surprising vistas of emerald vegetation and endless fields of *cardón* cacti. Although a steady stream of day-trippers now make the three-hour trek, Cachi still feels like yours to discover.

At Luna Cautiva, a café in an 18th-century adobe near the Iglesia San José, grab an outdoor table and snack on authentic *salteña* fare (fried empanadas, hearty goat stew) while surveying the scene on the cobbled streets of the tiny *centro*. A short walk from the Plaza 9 de Julio, the Mercado Artesanal is where you'll find vendors selling everything from *dulce de chayote* (a squash jelly) to hand-tooled leather bags and other artisan-certified

The pool at Estancia Colomé, 90 miles from Cachí, below.
Right: A guest room at La Merced del Alto. Opposite: Trail
riding at Estancia Colomé.

goods. Nighttime in Cachi is a laid-back affair—stop back at
Luna Cautiva for a traditional folk-music show *(peña)*, then
order a glass or two at nearby Oliver Wine Bar.

No trip to Cachi is complete without heading out into the
Andean foothills—and the best way to experience the vast
landscape is to wake up in it. Ninety minutes south of Cachi,
the Estancia Colomé embodies isolated luxury with nine
spacious, television-free suites surrounded by fields of lavender.
Farm-fresh dinners are served on a terrace with a *copa de vino*
from Colomé's 150-year-old vineyards. For those craving more
of a resort experience, La Merced del Alto lies just outside
of town, with a spa and pool surrounded by the panoramic
Nevado de Cachi mountains. +

For The Guide, see page 271.

A Trancoso local, left. Below: A cottage turned boutique on the Quadrado. Opposite: Drinks at Uxua Casa.

TRANCOSO

The beach town that time forgot

NEVER HEARD THE NAME? YOU'RE NOT ALONE. This destination is hardly on the global radar—at least not quite yet. A Pataxo Indian village turned Portuguese Jesuit enclave turned hippie dropout haven, Trancoso is one of the strangest and most beautiful places in Bahia, a sort of Brazilian Brigadoon.

On the Quadrado, or town square—five acres of unkempt grass, rimmed by a dirt footpath—paper lanterns hang from the branches of mango, tamarind, and cashew trees. Each evening, the lanterns are set alight, and the echoes of bossa nova fill the air. Couples and families stroll across the square, wearing Havaiana sandals or walking barefoot in the grass. It's that kind of place.

"Trancoso is where rich people from São Paulo go to pretend they're poor," jokes one visitor, and he's right: this 16th-century village has become a favorite retreat for wealthy Paulistas, looking for an antidote to their own mad metropolis. The "high season" lasts for just a few weeks around Christmas and New Year's, when the city's social whirl descends on Trancoso for a wild bacchanal. But for much of the year, all is strangely

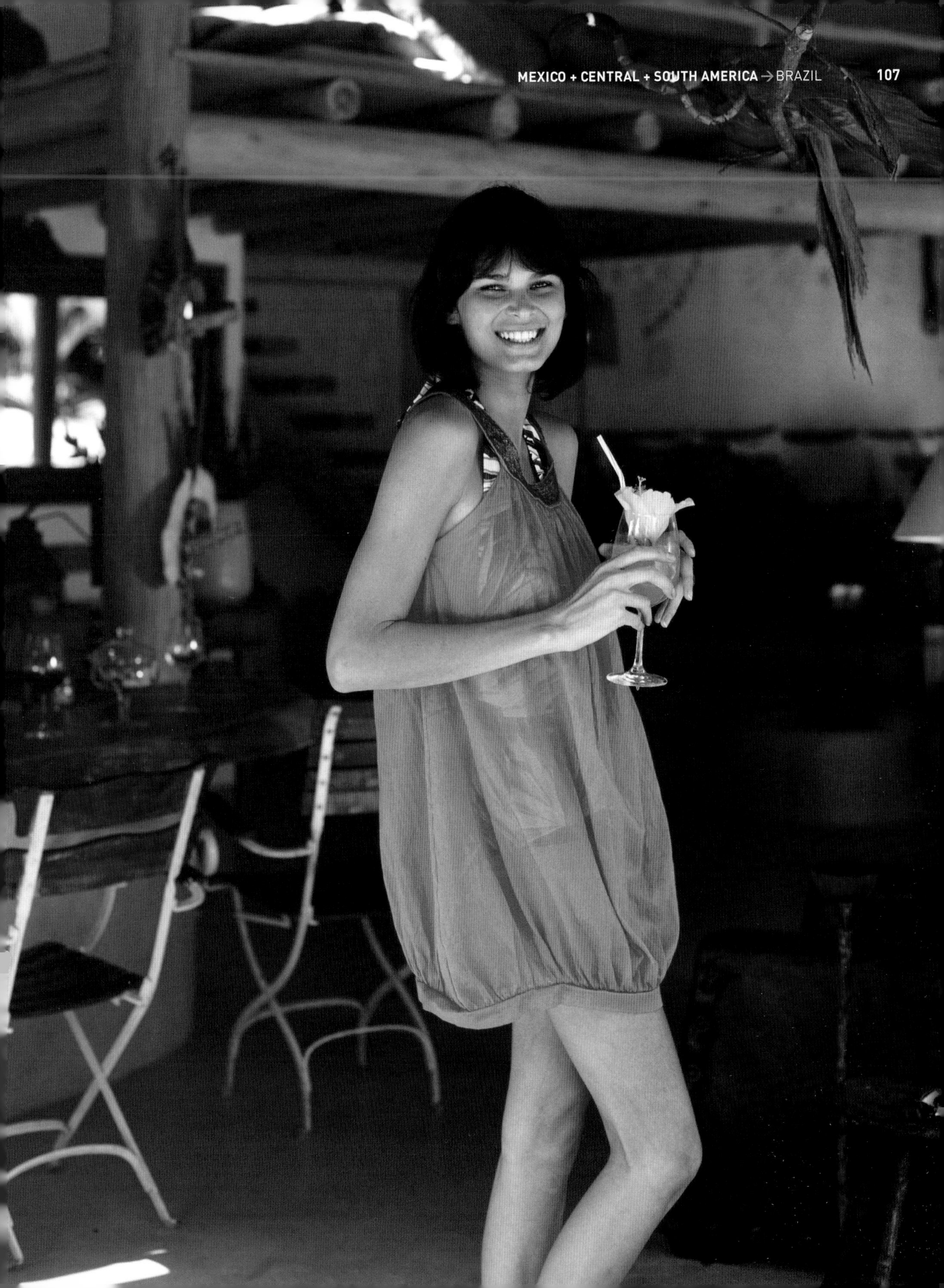

quiet, and visitors have the town and the beach to themselves.

For residents and travelers alike, life revolves around the Quadrado. At one end rises the Igreja de São João Batista, the second oldest church in Brazil, built by Portuguese settlers in 1586. Just behind it, a 1,200-foot cliff overlooks the translucent Atlantic and miles of sandy beach. Framing the square are 60 squat houses built from mud and clay, painted in brilliant hues from lime green to lavender. Many have been converted into artisans' workshops and restaurants; one candy-colored façade is a stunning new boutique hotel called Uxua Casa, the ideal setting for playing out your bohemian fantasy.

Beyond the Quadrado, there's not much to do or see in town, but that's exactly how visitors like it. During the heat of the day, when most shops are closed, folks make their way down to the shore—and what a shore it is. Trancoso lies at the heart of Bahia's Discovery Coast, along which runs a stretch of golden sand, much of it backed by nothing more than coconut

palms and towering red-clay cliffs. In either direction from town are at least a dozen distinct beaches, some accessible only by foot or by boat. (The best of them all: Praia do Espelho, or "Mirror Beach," about 20 miles south of town.) Rent a 4WD if you're feeling ambitious, but be warned: coastal roads are mostly unsealed and wend their way around tidal rivers, mangrove swamps, papaya plantations, and vast nature preserves. This is not a place to blaze through on a whirlwind trip. It's a place to slow down and enjoy at its own languid pace—one beach, one evening stroll, and one passion-fruit caipirinha at a time. ✦

For The Guide, see page 271.

A fisherman's hut on Praia dos Nativos. Opposite: Praia dos Coqueiros, another Trancoso beach.

EUROPE

Holland's 19th-century
Schalkhaar, one of Feather
Down Farms historic properties
in the U.K. and the Netherlands.

LONDON

**Vintage style takes
the town by storm**

Hope & Greenwood
in Covent Garden.
Opposite, clockwise
from top left: Geale
in Notting Hill;
shelves of goodies
Hope & Greenwood
Geales' take on
fish-and-chips;
sidewalk seating
at Geales; dressing
the part at Bourne
Hollingsworth; Hope
& Greenwood's old-
fashioned treats.

RETRO CANDY SHOPS AND A ROARING speakeasy scene? In London, what's old is new. The 1950's reign at Covent Garden's Hope & Greenwood, where the shelves are filled with crystal dishes of handmade confections and glass jars brimming with classic British sweets, from humbugs to giant gobstoppers. A soundtrack of jaunty jazz, displays of decorative antique tins, and packets of sweets labeled RATIONS add to the postwar whimsy. Across town in Notting Hill, the resurrected Geales, which first opened in 1939, draws families and fashionable types alike for upmarket beer-battered fish-and-chips—think haddock caught that day in Cornwall and a Ruinart Blanc de Blanc to wash it down. An original wooden specials board lists dishes of yore, such as mushy peas and shandy. At Treacle, open only on Sundays (and Saturdays during high season), the British teahouse tradition is alive and well; the goods include tea and ginger beer—no coffee!—and a selection of fairy cakes, Victoria sponges, and vintage tea caddies.

When night falls, the thing to do is swing. At Bourne & Hollingsworth, a stylish crowd downs gin fizzes and channels the spirit of madcap Pretty Young Things to the tune of big-band hits. Light-footed Londoners are also stepping into the Rivoli Ballroom for swing and rock-and-roll nights amid the original scarlet interior—all velvet draperies, flocked wallpaper, and oversize Chinese lanterns. Dress sharp and bring your best Fred and Ginger moves. ✛

For The Guide, see page 272.

THE COTSWOLDS

Rural yet impossibly glamorous

Fish-and-chips at Trouble House, near Tetbury, below. Right: The reflecting pools at Barnsley House. Opposite: Strolling through the Cotswolds village of Winchcombe.

IT WOULD BE HARD TO FIND A CHICER PLACE ON EARTH than the Cotswolds. In the last decade and a half, this 790-square-mile green zone—about three-quarters of which is covered by lush farmland—has seen a steady influx of weekending Londoners and celebrities: Kate Winslet, Elizabeth Hurley, Damien Hirst. There's even a growing number of full-time transplants, mostly former city dwellers chasing an upscale *Green Acres* dream.

Just about every Cotswolds village worth its *fleur de sel* has a Slow Food menu at its ancient pub or a contemporary bistro among its twee antique shops. Prince Charles gets a great deal of credit for spreading the green word—an elbow-to-elbow crowd flocks to his Highgrove Shop in Tetbury, which features his Duchy Originals organic goods. Chefs from London's restaurant scene continue to arrive. New-guard gastropub the Swan at Southrop (where Kate Moss is a regular) is currently overseen by Sebastian and Lana Snow, who garnered good reviews for their former establishment Snows on the Green. And 35-year-old Martin Caws owns and operates the cozy

Trouble House, near Tetbury; he ran Marco Pierre White's Mirabelle, on London's Curzon Street, before bundling off his wife and young son to the pastures in 2007.

At the Merriscourt Arts Centre, owner Tom Astor—who is, yes, from the English branch of *those* Astors—has brought a roster of small yet high-profile businesses to the stone houses on his enormous plot. They include a bespoke woodworking shop; the part-time studio of Jade Jagger's design partner, Tom Bartlett; an art gallery managed by curator Flora Fairbairn; a recording studio for the guitarist and composer William Lovelady; and a classic-car restoration outfit.

The area's modern boutique hotels fit right in. Despite its haute interiors, Barnsley House is laid-back and personal, with a friendly staff. The swinging Cotswolds88 Hotel may be on aesthetic overdrive, but the fare served in the dining room is predominantly local, including pork sausage and fresh pea soup. And the thoughtful touches at Cowley Manor (which looks straight out of a Knoll showroom, with a spa frequented by boldface names) include rows of wellies provided for guests. Without them, visitors couldn't tramp beside the two lakes on the property—and that would be a crime against nature. After all, in the Cotswolds, nature is still the main event.

For The Guide, see page 272.

The 17th-century limestone exterior of Barnsley House. Opposite: A sitting room at Cotswolds88.

One of Feather Down Farms' canvas tents.

ENGLISH COUNTRYSIDE

The ultimate agrarian vacation

THE SIMPLE LIFE NEVER SEEMED SO INVITING. At Feather Down Farms—small-scale rural enterprises throughout the United Kingdom and the Netherlands—you can play at homesteading, 18th-century style. The 22 preservation-minded properties, scattered across working farms, are an innovative way to experience the countryside and its down-home charms. Your lodging: an old-fashioned three-room canvas tent with comfortable beds, wooden floors, oil lamps, and a flushing loo. Rise with the roosters and spend your days visiting the flocks (everything from llamas to lambs), gathering eggs, and setting off to small villages by bike. At Lancashire's Dolphinholme Farm or Somerset's Moores Farm, you can cook a hearty stew of just-harvested produce on your own cast-iron stove; at Hampshire's Manor Farm, you can smoke a fresh organic chicken in a barrel. Ready for some back-to-the-earth pampering? Book a stay at Hollings Hill Farm in Herefordshire, where you can steep in an open-air, fire-warmed field spa. Go at night, under a sky spinning with stars—it's the best cure for an overworked soul. +

For The Guide, see page 272.

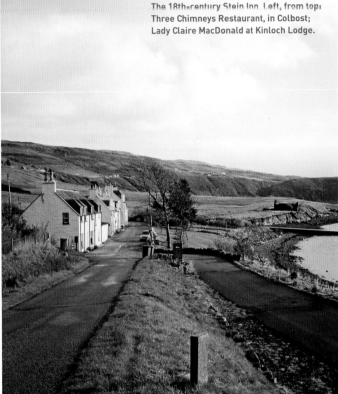

The 18th-century Stein Inn. Left, from top: Three Chimneys Restaurant, in Colbost; Lady Claire MacDonald at Kinloch Lodge.

ISLE OF SKYE

Scenic drama along a sleepy coast

SINGLE-LANE ROADS, SIGNS IN GAELIC, and mists swirling on mountains are what you'll find on this lobster-shaped island, just off Scotland's west coast. Three days is the right amount of time for a leisurely 204-mile driving route. The trip begins at the foot of the Trotternish Peninsula in the harbor town of Portree. In Colbost, on the Duirinish Peninsula, you'll find Three Chimneys Restaurant, a former crofter's cottage; the adjoining hotel, House Over-By, has rooms with sea views.

Take your time exploring the island's wild northwestern corner. From the Fairy Bridge on the Waternish Peninsula, a one-lane road follows the coast to the village of Stein, where the 18th-century Stein Inn stocks more than 125 varieties of single-malt whisky. At the Talisker Distillery, in Carbost, see how copper stills transform spring waters into headier stuff. End at Kinloch Lodge in Sleat, where cookbook author Lady Claire MacDonald has held court for more than three decades. In the formal dining room, she serves dishes such as apple and calvados cheesecake with warm caramel sauce—a delectable reward at journey's end. +

For The Guide, see page 273.

The pint of choice at McGarrigles Pub, in Sligo, left. Below: A bartender at the pub.

IRELAND

Tradition and change in the country's wild west

THE DRIVE THOUGH GLENGESH PASS IS HAIRY AND MAGNIFICENT—full of sharp curves, crazy dips and climbs, and head-spinning views. It's a fitting introduction to Glencolmcille, in the coastal highlands of County Donegal, where boggy pastures lead to a 6,000-year-old ring fort and a row of megalithic graves.

South of County Donegal lies Sligo, a provincial town enjoying its moment of growth. The striking Glasshouse Hotel is one recent addition, all bright colors and modern angles amid the 18th- and 19th-century buildings along the river Garavogue. But at McGarrigles Pub and the jam-packed Shoot the Crows, it's tradition—in the form of Irish music—that rules the day;

At the crossroads in Ballyvaughan, below. Right, from top: Outside Matt Molloy's pub, in Westport; along the coast of County Clare.

many of the tunes are authentic County Sligo standbys, both lilting and hard-driving. Masters of the art perform at the Ceolaras Coleman Music Centre, a 120-seat concert hall with classrooms and a small shop, 40 miles south in the village of Gurteen. And a lonely drive through the wilds of coastal West Mayo brings you to Matt Molloy's pub in Westport, owned by the flute player of the Chieftains and famous for its virtuoso trad sessions.

The route from Westport to Galway takes you through Connemara—a mountainous region where the bogs are boggier, the crags craggier, the silence more profound.

Once in County Clare, head to Ballyvaughan and the Corcomroe Abbey, a 12th-century Cistercian complex whose deep sense of history and remoteness is undiminished despite the brand-new cookie-cutter bungalows down the road. That's the beauty of this part of Ireland: the more things change, the more they (thankfully) stay the same. ✦

For The Guide, see page 273.

Notre Dame, one of Paris's iconic sights. Left: Chef Julien Duboué outside Afaria. Opposite: Afaria's roast duck breast, offal, and *frites*.

PARIS

Eating like a king for less

GOOD NEWS FOR BUDGET-WISE GOURMANDS: finding an affordable meal in Paris has never been easier. And though you might have to ditch the foie gras and the postprandial Armagnac, you'll get inventive, satisfying food at intimate restaurants packed with savvy locals.

One secret to eating better for less? Forget the words *à la carte*. The prix-fixe dinner at André Le Letty's L'Agassin, in the Seventh Arrondissement, might include garlicky escargots on a backdrop of parsley purée, or a meaty fillet of cod in a lake of light, modern beurre blanc. At Itinéraires, in the Latin Quarter, the blackboard menu echoes Spanish *nueva cocina*. Then there's the rightfully mobbed Afaria, in the up-and-coming 15th Arrondissement, which is prime territory for well-priced restaurants. Striped Basque runners on tables and a wine list scrawled on distressed mirrors set the mood for chef Julien Duboué's playful exuberance: a cheeky boudin noir "napoleon" richly layered with apples; a whole *magret*, or duck breast, baked on a bed of grape leaves atop a clay roof shingle. The place has become something of a hot spot for famous Parisian chefs—and why not? They love a good deal just like everyone else. ✦

For The Guide, see page 273.

THE PYRENEES

Follow the herd to greener pastures

IN THIS SLEEPY CORNER of the Couserans, a network of valleys in the French Pyrenees, an age-old tradition takes place: the annual walking of the herds up to their warm-weather mountain pastures. It's called the *transhumance*, and it might very well be the earliest form of summer travel. These local migrations happen all over Europe—in the Alps, the Apennines,

Corsica, Switzerland, and Spain. Here in the Midi-Pyrénées region of Ariège, visitors can join 10 different day hikes that accompany the animals into the hills. You can walk with native black Merens horses, hundreds of Gascon cows, or a thousand Tarasconnais or Castillonais sheep. You can hire a donkey to carry your child and pay for a post-hike barbecue dinner.

The day begins at 7 a.m. in a field outside of town, where a crowd equipped with hiking boots and daypacks begins to gather. By 8 a.m. the mist lifts, and the first flock of sheep starts marching up the road. The destination: a mountain

Clockwise from above: Pyrenees folk garb; a mountain hamlet; a villager from the region.
Opposite: A shepherd with his flock.

pasture, or *estive*, which could take five hours to reach. You'll
pass valleys of alpine flowers before breaking for lunch at the
Cirque de la Plagne, where four waterfalls plunge into a natural
amphitheater. Cured ham and cheese are only the precursors to
the main course: barbecued lamb chops (what else?).

Later in the day, the tourists head back down the valley to
farm stays or hotels like the romantic Château de Beauregard.
But for the shepherds, that's when the true work begins—the
long summer days on the mountain, watching sheep and sky. ✦

For The Guide, see page 273.

AIX-EN-PROVENCE

Classic pleasures in the south of France

Market day on the Place Richelme, in downtown Aix, above.
Right: Stacking chairs on the Cours Mirabeau. Opposite:
Dusky plums at the Place Richelme farmers' market.

YOU CAN SHOP MORNING, NOON, AND NIGHT IN PROVENCE—for croissants, baguettes, and newspapers; for tomatoes, peaches, string beans, strawberries, eggplants, mushrooms, and lettuce; for legs of lamb and chickens, cubes of beef and pork sausages. On the Place Richelme in downtown Aix-en-Provence stands the farmers' market to end all farmers' markets. It's not particularly big or fancy, but it is idyllic: busy from early morning until just after lunch, full of the hustle and flow of commerce. The vegetables, of course, are beautiful.

Aix is a former provincial capital built on a slope, with narrow cobblestoned streets that lead through various plazas. The town seems to carry you down the hill and toward its heart, the Cours Mirabeau, where two rows of tall plane trees and a series of fountains and cafés conspire to make you slow down and exhale. On a quiet street just off the Cours is the Four Dolphins fountain—each dolphin smiling and cheerful and with a slightly different expression, spouting thin streams of water into the basin below.

Forty minutes away, on the Mediterranean, is the picturesque fishing village of Cassis, with its

Above, clockwise from top left: The Cassis harbor, an easy daytrip from Aix; cafés along the Cours Mirabeau; Julia Child's kitchen in Plascassier. Opposite: The Four Dolphins fountain, in Aix.

dramatic coastline and dockside cafés. Also 40 minutes from Aix, and good for a lazy afternoon lunch: L'Hostellerie de l'Abbaye de la Celle, a small country inn and restaurant owned by Alain Ducasse. In this former 12th-century Benedictine abbey, prix-fixe tasting menus are served in a serene garden that invites you to linger. For a different kind of culinary immersion, Cooking with Friends in France offers classes at La Pitchoune, Julia and Paul Child's former vacation house in Plascassier, an hour and a half from Aix. The kitchen is still as Julia left it, with the outlines of her utensils stenciled on the Peg-Board wall. ✦

For The Guide, see page 273.

BASQUE COUNTRY

Culinary finds along the backroads

FRANCE'S PAYS BASQUE may not have the name recognition of its Spanish neighbor, with its higher-profile personalities and destinations (Arzak! Mugaritz! Bilbao!). But a handful of notable chefs and innkeepers—drawn to the region's agragrian lifestyle and gastronomic richness—have been shining a spotlight onto this untrodden corner of a well-trodden country.

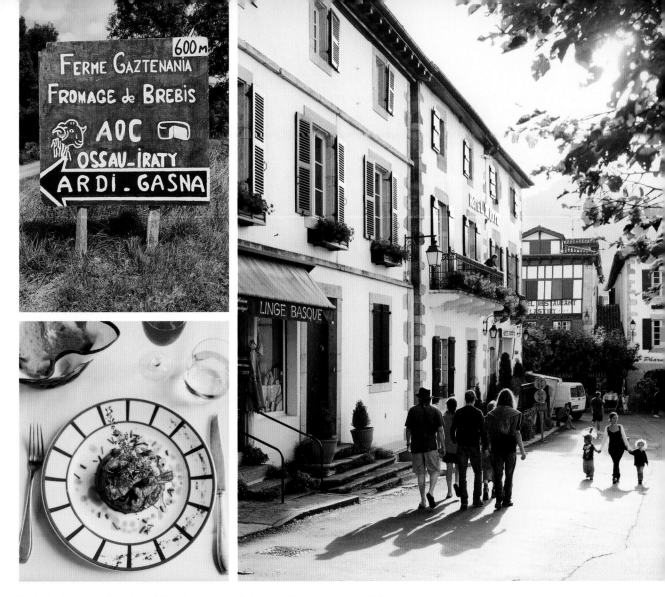

Clockwise from top left: A sign pointing the way to local sheep's-milk cheese; a street in Sare; Etche-Ona's prawn-and-tomato tart. Opposite: A view of the Pyrenées in Sare.

In the lovely village of Sare, the restaurant at the homey Hôtel Arraya sells fresh *gâteaux basques*—dense, mealy cakes filled with cherry preserves. Five miles away, in the town of St.-Pée-sur-Nivelle, is one of the best new dining experiences in southern France: L'Auberge Basque, a nine-room inn and restaurant run by 32-year-old Cédric Béchade, a protégé of Alain Ducasse. Béchade's dishes mix the flavors of the region with a host of global references—like the custard of creamy *brebis* (sheep's milk) and foie gras topped with a velouté of spring peas and tiny honey-cider croutons.

To the east lies Espelette, home to the russet-colored *piment d'Espelette*, a common ingredient in Basque cuisine. (Seek out the tiny Chocolatier Antton for ganache bonbons spiked with the powder.) Five miles north of the Spanish border, in pilgrimage country, St.-Jean-Pied-de-Port is traditionally the last French rest stop on one of the Santiago de Compostela routes. Break for lunch at Etche-Ona, where the food is light and sophisticated: a zingy gazpacho laced with dollops of basil sorbet; a tart of Ossau-Iraty cheese accompanied by tomato salad and huge grilled prawns.

Settle in for the evening at Hegia, a Michelin-starred

Dressed in traditional Basque style in
Sare, above. Right: Suite No. 1 at L'Auberge
Basque, in St.-Pée-sur-Nivelle. Opposite:
A breakfast table at Hegia, near Hasparren.

restaurant and guesthouse just outside
the town of Hasparren. If Hegia's
18th-century timbered exterior is a
monument to the traditional Pays
Basque, the interior is a testament to
its bold new wave. Each of the five
rooms is contemporary yet cozy (as in
a poured-concrete bathtub underneath
300-year-old rafters). Downstairs in
the kitchen, chef Arnaud Daguin—the
progeny of a venerated Gascon food family—uses only the
barest of embellishments to express the ingredients' full flavor.
Tender duck breast arrives over finely julienned carrots, pan-
cooked to a sweetened softness; delicate fillets of steamed hake
are served atop a sort of candied vegetable hash made of
slow-roasted beets and turnips. Wake early the next morning
to admire the purity of the Basque hills. There's hardly any
noise—just the breeze bearing the *tong-tong* of cowbells across
the fields. ✦

For The Guide, see page 273.

Foie gras con ceviche de tomate at DiverXo.

MADRID

Challenging Barcelona's restaurant supremacy

FROM ENDEARINGLY DOWDY TO SLEEK AND WORLDLY, Madrid has gotten a dramatic makeover—and so has its dining scene. More restaurants seem to have opened in the past few years than in the entire decade before. One of the best is DiverXo, from 29-year-old wunderkind David Muñoz (Madrid's answer to media darling David Chang, chef of New York's Momofuku empire). Adventurous epicures now flock to Muñoz's 20-seat spot in the drab Tetuán neighborhood for dishes that juggle Iberian, Asian, and Latin American flavors—like a potato tortilla filled with a quail egg and onion confit, in a chile and red-bean emulsion with a chaser of Chinese white tea.

Clockwise from top left: Madrid's Plaza de la Villa; Zaranda's chef, Fernando P. Arellano (center), with his kitchen team; the dining room at Zaranda.

At Zaranda, chef Fernando P. Arellano's voluptuous modern-Mediterranean menu includes a crispy-skinned suckling pig served over caramelized Chinese cabbage choucroute. At Kabuki Wellington, chef-owner Ricardo Sanz devises ingenious maki rolls around *huitlacoche* (corn fungus) and Galician Arzúa cheese. But ceviche may be the new sushi, if the popularity of Astrid & Gastón Madrid is any indication—try the *clásico* sea bass with lime juice, sweet potato, and corn. Regulars of the white-hot celebrity magnet Sula chase chorizo croquettes with champagne at the ground-floor tapas bar. An adjacent shop sells Joselito charcuterie (from the brand behind the world's greatest *ibérico* ham); the main restaurant serves variations on traditional stews along with chef Quique Dacosta's more high-minded culinary creations. Order a bacalao salad before moving on to one of Dacosta's neo-paellas. Then again, you could just get a bottle of Vega Sicilia and a *ración* of Gran Reserva Joselito *jamón* and wait for Penélope Cruz to show up. +

For The Guide, see page 274.

RIOJA

**New sights and an
an age-old ritual**

The modern tapas experience at Electra Rioja Gran Casino, above. Opposite: A bar crawl in the heart of the Casco Viejo.

UNLIKE TUSCANY OR BURGUNDY, the Rioja is a work in progress. Over the past two years, the Frank Gehry–designed hotel and tasting room at the Marqués de Riscal winery has transformed the area into an international destination, attracting a different caliber of visitor to this part of Spain. Gehry isn't the only one changing the landscape. Architects Santiago Calatrava, Zaha Hadid, and the emerging Basque standout Iñaki Aspiazu Iza have also designed wineries; many visitors now travel here specifically for the design. At the same time, an astonishing 500 new wineries have come alive in the past two decades. And the area now teems with ambitious chefs who are eager to lead a culinary revolution.

But despite the $100 bottles of wine and spectacular architecture, the Rioja remains a bastion of unpretentiousness. Sleepy Logroño, its only urban center, embodies the spirit of Spain's tapas tradition. (Spaniards well know that eating tapas in Logroño isn't the cutting-edge experience it is in San Sebastián or the traditional one it is in Seville, but it's infinitely more fun.) In the Casco Viejo, or old city, a jumble of bars and small shops that

are shuttered by day comes alive as the skies darken. Dozens of wine bars offer specialty plates and a list of by the glass regional selections that cost merely a dollar or two. Locals head out after work to catch up with friends over snacks and a few glasses of *tinto* or *rosado* that, likely as not, was made by someone they know. (The favored spots for an evening jaunt: Electra Rioja Gran Casino, Blanco y Negro, Bar Sebas, and Bar Soriano.) A few hardier souls might move on to a restaurant dinner. But usually it's enough to eat and talk for a couple of hours and then head home—gobbling up a grilled anchovy here and a bit of rabbit stew there; washing them down with wines that seem tailor-made for this purpose; tugging on the ties to local culture all the way. +

For The Guide, see page 274.

Bacalao with black-olive tapenade at Electra Rioja Gran Casino. Opposite, clockwise from top left: A street in the old city; bite-size quail at Electra Rioja Gran Casino; outside Bar Soriano; Bar Sebas before the evening rush.

DOURO VALLEY

Europe's next great wine destination?

PORTUGAL'S WINE INDUSTRY MAY BE BEST KNOWN FOR PORT, but times (and tastes) are changing. As the global hunt for the next big wine region heats up, the Douro Valley—a sunbaked landscape of circuitous roads along a narrow river gorge—has become the latest stop on Europe's oenotourism circuit.

The Salon de Musique at Quinta da Romaneira, left. Below: Quinta da Romaneira's private motorboat. Opposite: Quinta do Vallado.

Just outside Peso da Régua, the Quinta do Vallado winery overlooks the Corgo River from steep terraces, many of which were shaped by hand 300 years ago. Sixth-generation port- and winemaker João Ferreira Álvares Ribeiro converted the ground floor of his family's 18th-century manor into plain but comfortable guest rooms; this year, eight more suites were added in a new building amid the vines. During the past decade, his estate shifted much of its production to table wines, hoping to someday rival the demand for Pinot Noir from Burgundy or Napa Cabernet.

The poshest of the converted estates, the 1,000-acre Quinta da Romaneira, features two handsomely renovated manors—one with curlicue gates and a courtyard fountain, the other with an infinity pool and a tribal art collection. Lavish meals and wine tastings are held around the property throughout the day, with poems (in French, no less) handed out by the staff at studied intervals. Guests are taken on a cruise down the Douro River on a teak-and-fiberglass launch. This is the vineyard as luxury travel experience, with prices to match. At dusk, as the natural light disappears below the Douro Valley's craggy hills, candles illuminate the gravel paths of the quinta's grounds, leading the way back to your sleigh bed. +

For The Guide, see page 274.

LAKE COMO

Villa gardens in bloom

ARRIVE AT LAKE COMO'S VILLAS BY WATER—it's how visitors traveled in centuries past, and it's still the most dramatic way to get there. Board a water taxi in Bellagio (where the Grand Hotel Villa Serbelloni holds court), and in a single afternoon you can see three of the most exquisite estates along the shore: Villa del Balbianello, Villa Melzi, and Villa Carlotta.

Villa del Balbianello, owned and maintained by the Italian National Trust, lies on a peninsula that juts dramatically into the lake. The property reflects French, English, and Italian influences—all typical of the pleasure gardens of this period. At Villa Melzi, enormous old redwoods and water-craving swamp cypresses meet an allée of sycamore trees and a Moorish pavilion situated right at water's edge. Built around 1690, Villa Carlotta has an extensive collection of shrubs and trees, as well as what appears to be a stunning rain forest with numerous forms of exotica—ferns, giant magnolias, bananas, and orchids. Stroll the grounds and you're transported into a more dignified era—when a beautiful garden was a passion, not merely a piece of real estate. ✦

For The Guide, see page 274.

Clockwise from top: Villa del Balbianello; boxwood hedges at Villa Carlotta; a neoclassical bust among azaleas at Villa Melzi. Opposite: A pathway overlooking Lake Como at Villa del Balbianello.

VENICE

**Insider haunts in
the city of canals**

One of the Osteria Alle Testiere's nine tables, left. Above: The osteria's ravioli with shrimp, pumpkin, and ricotta. Opposite: Strolling across the San Paternian bridge.

VENICE HAS ALWAYS KNOWN HOW TO HONOR ITS PAST. It's the present—and future—that proves more difficult to negotiate. Yet the city manages to defy being characterized as a historical amusement park: witness the pedestrian bridge by Santiago Calatrava that spans the Grand Canal. In her sleek boutique, Madera, architect Francesca Meratti brings Venetian design into the 21st century with minimalist aprons, contemporary porcelain teapots, and her own line of finely sculpted wooden bowls. And avant-garde shoemaker Giovanna Zanella crafts custom footwear ranging from frog-skin flats to lace-up boots in green and pink leather.

Step into even the smallest of ateliers, and you'll find craftsmen working just as they would have generations ago. On the Campo de' Fiori, the owners of 63-year-old Legatoria Polliero create unique handmade papers using a collection of 300 antique Asian printing blocks. "Seafoam green" and "Rembrandt rust straw and silvery gold" are just a few of the poetic names legendary designer Mariano Fortuny would give his fabrics, on view at the Fortuny Factory and Showroom. Take a guided tour at the textile workshop of Tessitura Luigi Bevilacqua—a frequent source of inspiration for fashion and costume designers—to see how weavers create velvets on 18th-century looms.

For a taste of Venice's culinary traditions, book a much-coveted table at the 22-seat Osteria Alle Testiere.

Ca' Sagredo's Presidential Suite, above.
Right: A salon in Ca' Sagredo.

Sommelier Luca di Vita presides over the tiny *salotto*, outfitted with an antique marble-topped bar, where he advises patrons on pairing the best Venetian whites. Planning a picnic by the lagoon? Stock up on provisions at the recently opened Pronto Pesce Pronto. The delicatessen specializes in platters of seafood to go—like spiced couscous with mussels, and swordfish croquettes. Before taking shelter for the evening, make the obligatory visit to Harry's Bar. The crowds may be overwhelming, but people-watching doesn't get much better than this:

the 1931 venue is a favorite of A-listers, especially during the Venice Film Festival each September.

The grand hotels around the Piazza San Marco have had few rivals over the years. But a host of elegant new properties promise impeccable service, often at a more affordable price. Opposite the Church of the Frari, a narrow path behind a wooden door leads you through a brick-walled garden full of magnolias and olive trees to Oltre il Giardino, a stylish six-room villa. At the regal Ca' Sagredo, a 42-room palazzo dating back to the 15th century, the entrance is marked by an elaborate marble stairway and a fresco of *The Fall of the Giants* by 18th-century Rococo master Pietro Longhi. And at the four-room IQs, a hidden gem of a hotel, guests are lulled to sleep by the opera-singing gondoliers on the nearby canal. +

For The Guide, see page 274.

Inside Ca' Sagredo's
15th-century hall.

ROME

Basking in the holiday spirit

WHAT COULD FEEL MORE LIKE CHRISTMAS than a trip to the Pope's home turf? Stay at a hotel in a converted 17th-century cloister or a convent that takes paying guests, and a holiday trip to Rome becomes a good way to tap into tradition—no matter what your religious beliefs.

On a narrow street in Trastevere, the clay-roofed Hotel Santa Maria might conjure up images of friars silently gliding across the pebbled courtyards. But there's nothing monastic about the suites, which have multiple flat-screen TV's and walls freshly stenciled with vines. Join the crowds on a pilgrimage to the vast St. Peter's Basilica, and make your way up to the lofty dome ($10 per person via elevator, or $8 to hoof it up 323 spiraling, wedge-shaped steps). Due east is the next destination: the Piazza Navona Christmas festival, full of carnival games and vendors hawking spicy sausages. The air is thick with the sugary scent of the flat doughnuts called *fritelle*—the Italian equivalent of funnel cake.

St. Peter's Square, in Vatican City.

The square-domed Great Synagogue, one of Rome's most prominent Jewish historical sites, below. Right, from top: The church of Santa Brigida, next to the convent-guesthouse; fruit at the farmers' market on Campo de' Fiori. Opposite: Outside Hotel Santa Maria.

In the Centro, the convent and guesthouse of Casa di Santa Brigida was named for a Swedish saint (whose hip bone is enshrined in a reliquary on the premises). Yes, silver crucifixes and needlepoint Madonnas hang over the twin beds, but in many ways the still-working convent is just like any number of little pensiones. It's certainly well situated—only a block to the Campo de' Fiori, with its open-air market, and walking distance to Rome's Ghetto Vecchio, the historical Jewish quarter. A short distance away you'll find the boisterous Da Baffetto pizzeria and the old-fashioned gelato parlor Giolitti, where servers in white jackets with gold-braid epaulets scoop cones of *amaretto* and *stracciatella*.

Though it's said that only three percent of Italians attend church these days, midnight mass at Santa Maria in Trastevere is sure to be a packed house. On Christmas morning, all of Rome sleeps in—a lovely, low-key way to celebrate the holiday. ✢

For The Guide, see page 275.

THE CILENTO COAST

Diamond in the rough

TO CALL THIS THE ANTI-AMALFI isn't much of an exaggeration. The Cilento Coast lacks the manicured glamour, scene-y restaurants, and starry hotels of its counterpart across the Gulf of Salerno. And that's a good thing: thanks to its low profile, this portion of southern Italy has remained truer to its origins. The water here is some of the cleanest in the country; sun-worn fishermen still put out at dawn each day with their *menaiche*, or traditional hand-woven nets. The medieval fortress town of Castellabate is a UNESCO World Heritage site. Paestum, on the Sele

Mozzarella di bufala wrapped in myrtle leaves, left. Below: Inside the B&B Il Cannito. Opposite: The basilica at Castellabate.

Plain, has some of the best-preserved Greek temples on the Mediterranean. And, this being Italy, a gastronomic heritage flourishes; its cornerstones are the venerated *mozzarella di bufala campana* and *fichi bianchi dottati*, succulent lime-size white figs that grow in the hills around Mount Stella. You'll find them on the menu—along with a staggering seafood catch—at both the low-key U' Mazzeno, on the road to Punta Licosa, and Ristorante Il Caicco, with its garden terrace suspended almost a thousand feet above the sea in Castellabate.

Palazzo Belmonte, a rakishly elegant hotel with palm-shaded gardens on the Castellabate harbor, is no longer the only deluxe place to rest your head. In the hills above Paestum, local chef Anna Maria Barlotti Gorga opened Il Cannito, a four-room bed-and-breakfast spread across two houses dating back to the 13th century. The property evokes that kind of pared-down, old-meets-new look found in the pages of Italian shelter magazines: whitewashed rough-hewn beams and contemporary art, wide terraces of bone-colored travertine shaded by 300-year-old oaks. Dinners of freshly made pasta and garden-fresh produce are served from Gorga's streamlined professional kitchen, which is separated from the dining area by electronic sliding glass doors fitted into the centuries-old walls. Best of all, Il Cannito is just down the road from the bottega Tenuta Vannulo—where lines start at 8 a.m. for its legendary mozzarella, made only two hours before. +

For The Guide, see page 275.

In the fields of Madulain, left. Below, from top: Cycling through the center of old S-chanf; snacks for sale at a dairy near Pontresina.

THE ENGADINE VALLEY

A timeless family escape

THE ALPS, ESPECIALLY IN SUMMER, deserve their storybook reputation. There are lakes and medieval castles; meadows filled with wildflowers; trains winding through mountain tunnels; fresh milk, cheese, and, of course, chocolate. Perhaps the grandest of the Swiss alpine valleys is Engadine, in the southeastern canton of Graubünden—a fine place for an all-ages vacation.

Rent a house in the tiny village of Madulain and stock up on provisions from the supermarket in Samedan—from whole-wheat bread and tubes of Thomy mustard and mayonnaise to the creamy fruit-flavored ricotta called Quark. Or book a room at the Hotel Castell, in Zuoz, where the enormous breakfast buffet (in typical mountain-resort fashion) includes everything from salami to muesli to sweet rolls. Grab a set of wheels at Willy Sport and cycle down cobblestoned streets lined with centuries-old buildings whose walls are covered in *sgraffito*, a style of drawing in plaster that dates from the Renaissance. The bike path leads to the well-preserved village of S-chanf, where you can stop for schnitzel and fries at an outdoor café.

Picnicking in a mountain meadow is an essential part of the Engadine experience. At the Alp-Shaukäserei Morteratsch, a dairy near Pontresina, kids will be captivated watching workers stir a gigantic pot of curds over a fire. Add a round of cheese to your backpack and embark on a hike down the valley. You'll find the perfect spot to break for lunch along Lake Sils—where looming mountain peaks, their sharp ridges etched into the sky, hover over sloping green meadows like a scene from a vintage Swiss travel poster. ✢

For The Guide, see page 275.

For The Guide, see page 275.

Lake Sils, a prime picnicking spot in the Engadine Valley.

A server at the Schönburg Castle Hotel, below.
Right: A view of Schönburg's courtyard.

THE RHINE VALLEY

Ambling through the Middle Ages

ONE OF THE MOST HAUNTINGLY ROMANTIC
places in Europe, Schönburg Castle
Hotel commands the Rhine Valley
with a sphinxlike gravitas. Throughout
medieval times, it was a residence
for wealthy nobles; during the 17th
century, it was set on fire by the French
Army; and in the 1950's, after being
abandoned for more than 200 years, it
was turned into a hotel. Inside, spiral
staircases lead to medieval parapets
overlooking the vineyards that line the
winding river.

The castle makes a good first night's stay on a three-day
drive through the Middle Rhine. Nearby, at the Historische
Weinwirtschaft (Historical Wine Inn), a stone-walled restaurant
with a beamed ceiling, the tables are fashioned from old
wooden beds; it's the very essence of *Heimat*, the peculiarly
German nostalgia for connection with home and homeland.
The road south takes you to the university town of Heidelberg,
where the 12th-century Heidelberg Castle looms high on a hill.
East of Heidelberg, at the town of Neckarzimmern, break for
coffee and cake at Hornberg Castle, an 11th-century keep (and
now a hotel) with a view of the red-roofed village below.

The walled city of Rothenburg ob der Tauber is a medieval
time capsule of half-timbered houses and arched gateways.

The Hornberg Castle cafe, below. Left: Bratwurst and salad at the hotel's restaurant.

You can stay at a storied old pile called the Hotel Eisenhut, made up of four 15th- and 16th-century mansions just off the main square. In the Restaurant Mittermeier's busy basement *enoteca*, however, the vibe is hip and lively, with dark walnut tables full of stylish young locals. Head north on the Romantische Strasse, through orchards brimming with apples and pears, and you'll leave the Middle Ages behind as you reach Weimar, where the Bauhaus movement was founded in 1919. Park yourself at the 314-year-old Hotel Elephant, which you'd never guess—judging by its modern, urbane interiors—was once the meeting spot of choice for intellectuals like Goethe. ✦

For The Guide, see page 275.

Inside architect Norman Foster's
glass-and-steel Reichstag dome.

BERLIN

The new crucible of world culture

EVERYONE IS HERE—artists and hipsters and restaurateurs; writers and intellectuals; filmmakers and techno musicians; curators, actors, and architects. Berlin is an electrifying international scene, where a 21st-century brand of unpolished, after-hours glamour thrives under the weight of 20th-century history.

Since the collapse of the Wall, the city has been in mad flux, but now its physical infrastructure has more or less taken shape. The results of the building boom have admittedly been uneven. The Reichstag, with its transparent Norman Foster–designed dome and collection of contemporary art (like Gerhard Richter's stunning interpretation of the German flag), is a blessing upon the urban grid. But Potsdamer Platz, Berlin's commercial heart, might bring to mind a rouged-up version of the skyline in Raleigh, North Carolina.

Figuring out the neighborhood of the moment is like trying to corner an especially smart chicken, but one thing is certain: it's the formerly uncool western areas, like beautiful Kreuzberg, that now attract the creative class. Kreuzberg is also where Turkish and bohemian Berlin meet, making the city feel as multicultural as Paris or London. On a Tuesday or Friday, the Turkish Market is the place to sample a smorgasbord of fat navel oranges, hot spinach böreks, and glowing aubergines, surrounded by Anatolian women in sequined chadors. A walk west along the Landwehrkanal brings you to the restaurant Defne (which serves the spiciest octopus in town) and the nearby Ankerklause, a bar boat that becomes a free-for-all after sunset.

A Berliner in front of the Brandenburg Gate, above. Opposite: The Kaiser Wilhelm Memorial Church, whose damaged belfry was preserved as a testament to the devastation of war.

Berlin lives by its nightlife; even the average cabbie knows the score and will tell you that "Tresor is over and Café Moskau is full of teenagers," but Berghain is still the place to go. And then there's the KMA 36 bar, where the vodka martinis are excellent, and the architecture alone is worth the visit—this former GDR cosmetics studio is an open constructivist glass box that would rank with the best of Warsaw Pact design.

History is everywhere in Berlin. Tributes to its tragic past include the Kaiser Wilhelm Memorial Church, rebuilt at its original site on Breitscheidplatz after World War II with its damaged belfry preserved; and the thousands of concrete slabs that form the Memorial to the Murdered Jews of Europe, a stone's throw from the Brandenburg Gate. Modern Berliners are nothing if not earnest, genuinely caring about the communities they have forged out of the rubble of the 20th century's most problematic metropolis. The new Berlin is about its youth—and its youth are ready for anything. ✦

For The Guide, see page 275.

THE NETHERLANDS

Blazing a path between the stylish and the sustainable

RECYCLED DESIGN: THE LATEST FAD, or a movement in the making? In the Netherlands, there's no doubt about it—innovators are reveling in reuse. Tucked between the smoke shops in Amsterdam's Red Light District, De Bakkerswinkel bakery is outfitted with the scrap-wood furniture of Piet Hein Eek, one of Holland's biggest design stars. Eek's unselfconscious pieces—massive painted cupboards, here stocked with jars of jam and freshly baked breads and cakes—are as seductive as they are sustainable. Because his output is so limited, his works

(like the signature Scrap Wood Table, which costs around $10,000) are sold only in a handful of shops in Europe, like Amsterdam's Frozen Fountain and Rotterdam's Galerie Animaux.

A small city of broad canals and clanging church bells 45 minutes from Amsterdam, Utrecht is home to the studio of Tejo Remy, one of

Clockwise from left: Outside Galerie Animaux, in Rotterdam; a canal in Utrecht; Tejo Remy's *Accidental Carpet*. Opposite: Piet Hein Eek's table at Amsterdam's Frozen Fountain.

the country's brashest design talents. Lamps made out of milk bottles hang from the ceiling; what looks like a box of melted crayons spilling across the floor is actually Remy's *Accidental Carpet*—a rug too gorgeous to step on, made from old wool blankets sliced into strips, then folded and glued together.

An hour away from Utrecht, in the port city of Rotterdam, Studio Hergebruik (Studio Re-Use) features a motley collection of ideas. But amid the bags made out of bicycle inner tubes and the shelving system built inside an open coffin, you'll find a few treasures: vinyl records molded into fabulous pencil holders, and a chandelier made of plastic-bottle bottoms that could easily double as 60's Op Art. In this hyperdesigned country, recycled objects—with their rough edges and cheeky wit—are a way to reinvent the world. +

For The Guide, see page 276.

COPENHAGEN

Reinventing the waterfront

Clockwise from top left: A walkway at the Royal Danish Plahouse; a bird's-eye view of the waterfront; a bridge over the Inner Harbor. Opposite: The Black Diamond library extension.

ON A WARM AFTERNOON AT THE DOWNTOWN HARBOR, Copenhagen feels like an ancient city glorying in its youthful vigor. Students and professionals wheel by on bicycles; canalside cafés spill over with people drinking Tuborg beer. This famously pedestrian- and bike-friendly city is now reclaiming its waterfront—a new phase for what may be the ultimate modern metropolis.

The challenge: how to channel the flow of street life and turn a former maritime highway into a kind of public square. One solution? High-end architecture such as Frøsiloen, a pair of massive silos now converted into apartments. Sinuous yet simple, the buildings are connected by a foot-and-bike bridge to Fisketorvet, a shopping mall in the former fish market. Cultural buildings are also used as magnets—pulling crowds toward the water and forcing the rest of the city to shift around them. The Black Diamond, with its concert hall and restaurant, is a glossy, crystalline extension to the Royal Library; the new Royal Danish Playhouse has a breathtaking glass wall that makes the theater feel like a maritime experience; and the Operaen, an opera house across the canal on a former navy pier, is a glass-and-steel egg beneath a silvery, wafer-like canopy. ✦

For The Guide, see page 276.

NORWAY

Say *hallo* to
the new north

IN MIDSUMMER, night never quite comes to Oslo, which lies on a sheltered estuary seven degrees latitude below the Arctic Circle. On an early-morning walk along Pipervika, the Norwegian capital's principal harbor, the sun is already at high-noon strength. Along the western flank, onetime shipyards have been turned into a popular outdoor dining area called Aker Brygge. You can practically feel the remoteness of this place by the crisp, arctic clarity of the warm air.

A little more than 40 years ago, Norway was one of the poorest corners of Europe. Now, thanks to a vast oil surplus, it has one of the highest standards of living in the world. But the locals are slow to change, clinging fast to Nordic traditions—especially a deep reverence for their surroundings. The architecture in Oslo reflects this element of the Norwegian character: solid rather than flashy, with heavy stone foundations. With the exception of the stunning new Opera House, much of Oslo looks more like parts of Eastern Europe than sleek Copenhagen. Yet in the boutique-filled neighborhood of Grünerløkka, stylish restaurants like Sult proclaim an edgy new side to the city; so does

From top: Cod with bok choy at Sult, in Oslo; the dining room at Oslo's Bagatelle; Godt Brød bakery, in Bergen.

Undredal, an archetypal Norwegian village,
on an offshoot of the Sogne Fjord.

the Michelin-starred Bagatelle, whose dining room (dominated by an Andreas Gursky photograph) is filled with the sound of boisterous conversation, tableware clinking, and people wholeheartedly indulging in the pleasures of food.

Explore the countryside by cruising around the fjords on the western coast, where steamers have been plying the route from Bergen to well above the Arctic Circle since the late 19th century. As Norway's charming second city, Bergen has a relaxed, youthful vibe that calls to mind an American college town. Students while away the afternoons on the lawns near the National Theater or over coffee at the Godt Brød bakery, one of the city's many popular cafés. Set sail from Bergen for the Sogne Fjord, the longest and deepest in Norway, where jagged, densely forested mountains rise up from waters so still and flat that they create a perfect reflection of the world above. Lost in an endless wall of forest, a solitary farmstead stakes its claim on the steep hillside. You'll understand why nature so captures the Norwegian imagination: this land was formed on a scale no man-made city can rival. ✦

For The Guide, see page 276.

BALTIC COAST

Buzzing beaches and an unspoiled island

THERE'S SOMETHING TOUCHINGLY OLD-WORLD about the coasts of Latvia and Estonia—Europe's lost Riviera, a region ripe for discovery. Jurmala, in Latvia, is the best-known beach resort on the Baltic. Its main promenade, Jomas Iela, sits next to Majori, the most popular beach, and is lined with buildings in a jumble of styles—from 19th-century wooden villas to minimalist Scandinavian architecture. At night, vacationing families dine at one of the many outdoor restaurants on the promenade, where you can buy ice cream and cotton candy, sit in a rowdy beer

A view of the Baltic Coast from Pädaste Manor's spa deck. Opposite: A dip in the Baltic Sea in front of the hotel.

Looking into Pädaste Manor, below. Right, from top: A Manor House suite at Pädaste; the rooftops of Tallinn, the Estonian capital, on the country's northern coast.

garden, or hop aboard a small-scale amusement park ride. Folks tend to dress for the nightly parade in a mix of halter tops and elegant evening wear: a display of finery that only adds to the sweetly retro atmosphere.

Even after becoming part of the European Union, the Estonian island of Muhu (a five-hour drive from Jurmala, and three hours from Tallinn, Estonia's capital) has seen few visitors and little in the way of development. On Muhu, Pädaste Manor was once the 19th-century home of German aristocrats—and is one of the few estate houses in the country that wasn't torn down during the Soviet era. Now it's a hotel, with thick old trees swaying high above a lawn and low stone buildings surrounding a pretty quad. Get into full hunter-gatherer mode at the manor's Sea House restaurant, whose menu includes roasted ostrich and moose carpaccio. Then book some time at the spa, which adheres to the Baltic philosophy that vacations should be curative, not just fun. Case in point: the hay treatment, which involves being wrapped in a giant grassy cocoon of gauze, lowered into a wooden vat of warm water, and left to steep. The ideal follow-up? A good old-fashioned goat's-milk massage. ✦

For The Guide, see page 276.

KRAKÓW
A nighthawk's tour

AT DUSK, KRAKÓWIANS GATHER in Rynek Głowny, Europe's largest medieval square—the prelude to an Old Town nightlife scene that hits its stride well after dark. Start the evening with dinner at Copernicus, a nine-table restaurant in a restored manor, where braised rabbit–filled pierogi go down all too easily with a shot of Wyborowa vodka. Then move on to Pauza, and don't be deterred by the shabby 19th-century tenement-house exterior—this is the spot of choice for Kraków's cognoscenti. You could spend an entire evening wandering from Pauza's art gallery to its basement nightclub and its lounge, which overlooks the skyline. Close to midnight, head to one of the city's signature cellar bars, such as Klub Kulturalny, whose bare stone walls give it the look of a grotto.

The narrow streets of Kazimierz, Kraków's old Jewish quarter, were once lined with kosher bakeries, delicatessens, and butcher shops. Today they're the site of the city's most distinctive bars and coffeehouses. British bachelor parties are rife here, but three venues manage to evade the stags: Zblizenia, a lounge with low couches that draws a sophisticated crowd; the Singer Café, where candles sit on top of sewing-machine tables; and the Moment Café, where 19th-century clocks cover the walls like an ode to the vanishing night. +

For The Guide, see page 277.

Clockwise from top: Old Town after dark; a clubgoer at Pauza; the club's dimly lit interior.

ST PETERSBURG

Live like a czar

THE FORMER SEAT OF IMPERIAL RUSSIA has a surreal beauty, especially when its fairy-tale architecture—the mint-green Winter Palace, the Church of our Savior on Spilled Blood—stands in sharp relief to the crystalline snow. The landmarks are worth a visit: the Hermitage Museum, the Summer Palace, and the Mariinsky Theater (which opened a $40 million concert hall in 2007). But save time to discover some local favorites. At the pan-Asian restaurant Terrassa, ask for a table on the balcony overlooking Nevsky Prospekt. The less-discovered Vasilievsky Island, west of the city center, is home to the low-lit Restoran, known for its house-infused vodkas and *pelmeni*, Siberian dumplings filled with ground elk meat. Spend the night in a suite at the Taleon Imperial Hotel, a favorite of Russian high rollers, or book a room at the recently restored Grand Hotel Europe. But to truly get in touch with your inner Romanov, splurge on an order of the Caspian Sea's finest at the Grand Hotel's Caviar Bar. Then take a trip to the Imperial Porcelain Manufactory, maker of fine-china tea sets for the country's aristocracy since 1744. Not feeling particularly flush? You can always opt for a gold-filigree shot glass. ✦

For The Guide, see page 277.

A panoramic view of
St. Petersburg's
University Embankment.

St. Basil's Cathedral, on Red Square. Opposite: The main dining room at Bosco Bar.

MOSCOW

A no-holds-barred feast

LONDON MINIMALISM, ROMANOV POMP, Tokyo appropriation, Cossack kitsch—it's all here in this brash, booming city that never stops eating, economic *krizis* or not. But you can forgive Moscow restaurants their theme park–like qualities: after all, it was less than 20 years ago that a dining-out culture re-emerged from long decades of Socialist shortages.

The latest homegrown hot spot is Stolovaya No. 57, a doting replica of a Communist-era workers' canteen within the ritzy GUM department store. Smoky pea soup and small, lacy blini fried in rich Vologda butter are served on grayish canteen-issue dishware, which customers clear themselves (a nod to the days of the "classless society"). Even the tourist traps have

A server in traditional Ukrainian costume at Shinok restaurant, below. Left, from top: The interior of Turandot; sturgeon kebabs with sweet dipping sauce at Barashka.

good food—like the pastas and salads served at Bosco Bar, with its prime Red Square tables facing St. Basil's candy-colored domes. Flaky *pirozhki* and almond croissants are on hand at the neo-Baroque Konditerskaya Pushkin; its sister restaurant, the eye-popping Turandot, serves fanciful dim sum in an atmosphere best described as Rococo on steroids. More Asian-inspired dishes, like tandoori duck and Kamchatka crab, can be had at Nedalny Vostok, where young dudes in Roberto Cavalli actually blend in with the slick interiors.

Turn back the clock with a spin through the kitchens of the former republics. For Georgia's spicy regional cuisine, hit the cavernous Genatsvale Arbat; for Azerbaijan's succulent sturgeon kebabs, there's the understated Barashka. Finally, for a taste of Ukraine, try the faux-farmhouse Shinok, where waitresses in embroidered blouses deliver earthenware pots of borscht and dense slices of rye bread draped with snow-white petals of cured lard. It's rustic cooking, done with finesse—a breath of fresh air in this bling-crazy capital. +

For The Guide, see page 277.

A trolley on Istanbul's Istiklal Cadessi, left. Below, from top: Babylon Lounge; the restaurant in the Marmara Pera hotel.

ISTANBUL

Bohemian life along the Bosporus

IT'S OFFICIAL: ASMALIMESCIT IS HAVING A MOMENT. This once-downtrodden part of Istanbul's central Beyoglu district now bustles with lively restaurants and music venues—especially on the lanes behind Tünel Square and the pedestrian-only Istiklal Caddesi. Yet the quarter still maintains the feel of old Istanbul, with its ancient façades and narrow streets.

One star of the new Asmalimescit generation: the boutique Ümit Ünal Doors, where eponymous neighborhood resident Ünal sells his avant-garde women's fashions. Babylon, one of Istanbul's foremost music spots, is still going strong—and has now branched out with Babylon Lounge, where concertgoers flock for smoked-salmon *pizzete* and pan-Mediterranean salads. Pizza is also a big draw at the two locations of Otto; at the Sofyali branch, you can also try the *votka gelincik*, a mix of vodka and a house-made syrup of poppy flowers. Bask in the neighborhood's after-hours energy by booking a room at the Marmara Pera, with views of the glittering city below. +

For The Guide, see page 277.

Views of the Nile from the steamship *Sudan*, traveling from Aswan to Luxor, Egypt.

AFRICA +
THE
MIDDLE
EAST

Casa Garcia restaurant in Asilah, Tangier's beach retreat, left. Below: Berber jewelry at Galerie Tindouf. Opposite: Textiles at Boutique Majid.

TANGIER

A shopper's secret haunt

ATTENTION, INTREPID BARGAIN HUNTERS: from kilims and textiles to antique furniture, a stunning variety of items await in Tangier, Morocco's northernmost city. Add a seaside stop at nearby Asilah, with its straw market and camels loping down the beach, and you have a shopping trip that feels like an exotic discovery.

Hidden up a flight of stairs, Tangier's Fondouk Chejra, or Weavers' Market, is a series of covered stalls where men spin wool on wooden wheels in a scene straight out of the 19th century. (One particularly unpretentious stall—literally a hole in the wall—does business with Barneys New York.) At the charmingly dusty, cluttered Galerie Tindouf, the bewitching wares—like vintage cushion covers with jewel-like

embroidery—run to the higher end of the price spectrum. For cheap but first-rate trifles, head to Marrakech La Rouge, where you'll find spice holders, hand-painted cups from Fez, inlaid boxes, miniature teapots, and more. Stack up a pile and haggle for the lot, a good-natured ritual that's an intrinsic part of the local culture.

Looking for a pair of utterly distinctive ankle boots? At Boutique Volubilis, in the Petit Socco, the

handmade, oddly colored booties—halfway between hobbit footwear and Comme des Garçons—are embellished with covered buttons and lacings. At Boutique Majid, the Ali Baba's cavern–like display includes carpets of bamboo and leather, massive amber bead necklaces, synagogue lamps, and an old camel rack. And it wouldn't be Tangier without a visit to a traditional rug store: the owners of Coin de L'Art Berbère provide Perrier while you browse an endless array of carpets, most of them underpriced. Retire with your purchases to the chic Hôtel Nord-Pinus Tanger, a *riad* in the city's heart, where you'll sleep surrounded by keepsakes both old and new. ✦

For The Guide, see page 278.

KENYA

A handcrafted tour

A Samburu woman making a lamp, left. Above:
Beaded baskets at Julia Francombe's workshop.
Opposite: Scarves at Anna Trzebinski's studio.

YOU CAN TELL A LOT ABOUT A WOMAN from her wardrobe. But for the Samburu tribeswomen on the dusty plains of Kenya's North Eastern Province, or their highland cousins, the Laikipiak Masai, clothes form virtual autobiographies: green beads connote grass or infants, red for blood or young women, white for purity. "There is a language to the beads," says Julia Francombe, who holds beading workshops and hosts guests on her family's farm, Ol Malo, at the edge of the Laikipia Plateau. "I can tell how many suitors she has had, how long she has been married, the sex of her children. Westerners have nothing like it."

The best way to experience these handicraft traditions is with a visit to a women's collective. Think of them as quilting bees with a purpose: in this remote society, women are gathering together and employing their skills to sustain welfare in a community where wealth still grazes on four hooves. Whenever other tasks—herding goats, fetching water, nursing babies—can

Women in handmade finery at Anna Trzebinski's Nairobi workshop, above. Opposite: A daybed at Lemarti's Camp, near the Laikipia Plateau.

be set aside, they create one-of-a-kind baskets, rugs, bracelets, shawls, and pottery to sell, all at remarkably affordable prices.

At the five-tent Lemarti's Camp, Anna Trzebinski (who also has a workshop in Nairobi) and her Samburu husband, Lemarti Loyapan, arrange meetings with beadworkers from the Laikipia Plateau. The women wear colorful cotton *shukas* knotted under layered chest plates of wire and beads, an ensemble that demands elegantly erect posture. Tarps are covered with their wares—*sayen enkwe* (headdresses) stitched with leather and plastic buttons; tanned goatskin bags; bracelets and neckbands. Often the workmanship is exceptional. Visits are unhurried, typically lasting until the sun drops down over the mountains. After the bartering is over and everyone is satisfied, the women disperse, striding out into the distance on sandals made from recycled tires. ✦

For The Guide, see page 278.

NAMIBIA

Stylish hideaways amid epic landscapes

BRAD PITT AND ANGELINA JOLIE are probably the reasons most Americans have heard about Namibia. A few years ago, this southern African country officially entered the pop culture lexicon when the couple stayed at a beach resort here while awaiting the birth of one of their children. But in fact, Namibia has been quietly coming into its own for the past decade. Along with magnificent scenery—deserts with thousand-foot sand dunes, a coastline strewn with ancient shipwrecks—it has some of the biggest yet least known game parks in Africa. Tourism is low-key, with the emphasis on smart, well-designed, environmentally sensitive lodges in remote areas.

At Little Kulala, on a 90,000-acre wilderness reserve near the colossal Sossusvlei sand dunes, the 11 villas have rooftop terraces with "sky beds" for stargazing. The lodge hosts guided desert drives, where you'll see giant dragonflies, spotted hyenas, and camel thorn trees hung with the monster nests of the sociable weaver (which can hold several hundred birds and last for up to a hundred years).

The main lodge at the Serra Cafema Camp sits on stilts above the

A private plunge pool at Little Ongava, in northern Namibia, above. Opposite: Gemsbok (African antelopes) roam the Namib desert.

Kunene River, which separates Namibia and Angola. Eight loftlike chalets are filled with carved Nguni furniture, with copper basins mounted on log pedestals in the bathrooms. Meals are sophisticated, including candlelit dinners of fish *en papillote* followed by chocolate mousse. The region is home to the Himba, a nomadic tribe whose women wear elaborately braided dreadlocks.

One of the country's most luxurious compounds, the three-cottage Little Ongava lies in the Ongawa Game Reserve, at the edge of northern Namibia's Etosha National Park. Interiors make extensive use of African artists' work: masks from Burkina Faso, wooden bowls from Zambia, Ethiopian trays, Congolese wall hangings, Namibian paintings. The ultimate prize, however, lies out in the bush—where you're likely to see packs of 8,000-pound white rhinos feeding on the foliage.

The Fort on Fisher's Pan is set within Onguma Game Reserve, a private 50,000-acre slice of Etosha National Park. It's an exotic structure—tall, thick walls; massive studded doors; multiple patios; secret staircases—at the edge of a large watering hole, where zebras assemble at sunset. During a four-hour excursion in the game park, you can expect to see giraffes, elephants, wildebeests, leopard tortoises, and the occasional lion. Aptly enough, Onguma means "the place you don't want to leave." +

For The Guide, see page 278.

Rooftop Airstream trailers at the Grand Daddy Hotel, left. Below: Works at Clementina Ceramics in the Old Biscuit Mill.

CAPE TOWN

A new face on the global design scene

EVERY SATURDAY MORNING in the neighborhood of Woodstock, through the entrance gates of the Old Biscuit Mill factory complex, South Africa's most eclectic eye candy is on show. A hundred-plus stalls peddle gorgeous food and even more gorgeous objects: handwoven espadrilles and bolts of block-printed cotton tea towels; free-trade coffee and piles of loose teas; organic biltong (Afrikaans beef jerky) and *chèvre frais* from Franschhoek. The cross section of humanity includes dreadlocked vendors, bronzed mothers from the suburbs, and kids in skinny jeans with asymmetrical haircuts. The scene may remind you of Brooklyn's Williamsburg, circa 2002.

Welcome to the Neighbourgoods Market—part of the rapidly developing Cape Town creative class. In Woodstock, a design and art collective called Whatiftheworld stages parties and gallery exhibits to promote the work of emerging South African talents. The fact that these up-and-coming designers are gaining traction isn't all that surprising once you've tapped into the city's

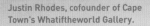

Justin Rhodes, cofounder of Cape Town's Whatiftheworld Gallery.

KIND POCKETS
RICHARD HART

Inside the Dorothy Airstream trailer at the Grand Daddy Hotel.

undeniable buzz. You can see the signs on Woodstock's side streets, in freshly converted warehouses that now house Web companies, antiques dealers, and nascent fashion lines. Along perennially chic Upper Kloof Street, in the well-heeled Gardens district, cafés are stocked with magazine racks of *Visi*, South Africa's design bible, as well as issues of *V, BlackBook,* and *Casa da Abitare*. Near Heritage Square, artists and art dealers converge over small plates in the courtyard of the wine bar Caveau. And at Brewers & Union, a beer bar–charcuterie, tribes of hipsters fill the front terrace in the after-work hours, clutching microbrews and nibbling at platters of salumi and butterfish carpaccio.

The innovative energy extends to the Grand Daddy, a new hotel with a rooftop collection of tricked-out Airstream trailers that serve as rooms. Each has a different tongue-in-cheek theme, from Afrofunked (teak paneling and low-slung sofas that recall a 70's conversation pit) to Love of Lace (a Priscilla Presley–esque fantasy of quilted pink satin and chandeliers). Edgy, fresh design that doesn't take itself too seriously: The world's latest style capital makes an auspicious debut. +

For The Guide, see page 279.

AFRICA + THE MIDDLE EAST · SOUTH AFRICA   **191**

Above, clockwise from top left: A cheetah on the Samara game reserve; the dining room at Karoo Lodge; an alfresco shower at the lodge.

SAMARA PRIVATE GAME RESERVE

Where the wild things are

VAST DOESN'T EVEN BEGIN TO DESCRIBE this landscape. In South Africa's Great Karoo region, Samara Private Game Reserve unfolds as far as the eye can see. Reintroduced springbok, eland, oryx, gemsbok, and endangered mountain zebra cavort on the 70,000-acre spread (which has four of the country's seven biomes, from mountain to savanna); game drives are spent tracking rare cheetah, with sightings virtually guaranteed. Base camp is Karoo Lodge, a 19th-century renovated farmstead filled with colonial antiques and artwork.

Activities aren't limited to the game drives. You can take a guided walk with a ranger and view fossils dating back 250 million years, or dine on rosemary-scented lamb in an open-air boma. The sky looms large, and the horizon seems endless: reality, as you know it, is another lifetime away. +

For The Guide, see page 279.

ALEXANDRIA

An ancient marvel reinvented

The waterfront Corniche boulevard, above. Right: The Biblotheca Alexandrina's computer area.
Opposite: The entrance to the library, featuring characters in 120 different languages.

AMID THE CRUMBLING BUILDINGS that line the beachfront of Egypt's second-largest city, the hypermodern reincarnation of the library of Alexandria looks as if it dropped down from outer space. The disc-shaped design, by Norwegian firm Snøhetta (which also created Oslo's National Opera House), resembles a high-tech rendition of the sun rising over the Mediterranean— or a massive computer chip lodged on the shore.

The library opened in 2002 on roughly the same site where its predecessor disappeared 1,600 years ago. (The exact cause of its destruction remains a mystery, though fire, earthquakes, or war likely played a part.) While the original served as classical antiquity's leading storehouse of knowledge, the Bibliotheca Alexandrina has an even more ambitious goal: to transform modern-day Egypt and the Islamic world. No small feat, in a country that limits press freedoms and censors books. But this is far more than a book repository—the complex also houses four museums, a planetarium, a children's science center, a library for the blind, and seven research institutes. It's already introducing technology considered cutting-edge everywhere else. And it provides access to materials that are normally off-limits in Arab countries, including the works of Salman Rushdie (albeit on request from closed stacks). Most importantly, thanks to more than 500 events a year, the Bibliotheca Alexandrina has become a gathering place for scientists, literary figures, and other thinkers from around the world. With this approach— centered on culture and intellectual freedom—the spirit of the original library of Alexandria lives on. ✦

For The Guide, see page 279.

THE NILE

THE *SUDAN* IS A PERFECT SHIP—the ship you dream of, on two tiers with 23 cabins and five suites, overlooking generous decks equipped with tables and wicker chairs from which to admire the slow-moving scenery. This steamship, which originally belonged to Egypt's King Fouad and has an engine that's more than 100 years old, is where Agatha Christie wrote much of *Death on the Nile*. There are few better vessels for a four-day cruise down the famous river, from Aswan to Luxor.

In the wood-paneled dining room, tables are set with white Flanders-cotton tablecloths and daily arrangements of

The steamship *Sudan*, docked in Aswan.
Opposite: A waiter on the *Sudan* wearing
the traditional tarboosh.

A captain on the *Sudan*, below. Right: The ship's viewing deck. Opposite: The Temple of Edfu, outside Luxor, one of the excursions on land.

fresh flowers. Meals are simple and delicious—meatballs or shawarma kebabs with rice and baked cauliflower, baby okra in tomato sauce, and homey desserts such as *mahallabiyya* pudding. The waiters wear stately maroon or navy djellabas with white arabesques down the middle, a wide sash at the waist, and a red tarboosh (as the fez is called in Egypt).

The *Sudan* runs as smoothly as its well-oiled pistons, which sit in an exposed well at the entrance for all to admire. On either side of the boat, large wheels churn the waters into white froth and heave the vessel gently along its course downstream. Excursions (which take place in the morning to avoid the heat) include the Nile Valley's major sights: the temples of Kom Ombo and Edfu, the Red Chapel of Queen Hatshepsut in the Open-Air Museum at Karnak. At the end of the third day, the boat reaches Luxor, where the Hotel Al Moudira beckons, an oasis of fragrant gardens and high-domed rooms. Yet as seductive as the attractions on land may be, it's spending time on the Nile that feels like the perfect activity— daydreaming, doing much of nothing, observing the rhythms of river life. ✦

For The Guide, see page 279.

TEL AVIV

A resilient Mediterranean metropolis

Revelers in Tel Aviv Port, left. Below: Tel Aviv's Cinema Hotel, a Bauhaus-era structure. Opposite: Frishman Beach, part of the city's three-mile stretch of sand.

ON VIBRANT ROTHSCHILD BOULEVARD, teenagers saunter by clutching cell phones, young parents push Mercedes-like strollers, and crowds cluster at open-air espresso bars. "What Mideast crisis?" the first-time visitor might ask after surveying the lively scene. The increased affluence and sophistication allow many pleasure-seeking residents of Tel Aviv to take refuge in a bubble, or what Israelis call *habuah*—a way of coping with the surrounding turbulence.

The nation's second largest city, Tel Aviv is the hub of culture, finance, and media. European-style shopping streets and innovative restaurants join glittering towers designed by Philippe Starck, I. M. Pei, Richard Meier, and Ron Arad. The

Bauhaus Foundation Museum, which opened in 2007, showcases original furniture by the likes of Mies van der Rohe and Marcel Breuer—an ode to a city that boasts the largest concentration of Bauhaus architecture in the world. (In 2003, it was named a UNESCO World Heritage site.)

Still, it's not hard to detect what lurks beneath the conviviality. *"Yesh l'chah neshek?"* ("Do you have a weapon?") ask the guards as they

Basking in the sun in the rehabilitated port district. Opposite: Air force cadets take a break at Azrieli Center, home to one of Tel Aviv's largest malls.

inspect bags at the entrances of stores, museums, restaurants, cafés, and just about every other public building in town. The nonchalant query is but one of Tel Aviv's vivid incongruities. Machine gun–toting off-duty soldiers window-shop along Sheinkin Street, where a kabbalah center sits next to the flashy Menz underwear boutique. At Frishman Beach, Orthodox Jewish men and women bathe on alternating days at a swimming area encircled by high walls; this enclave of modesty just happens to be near the gay beach, where a gym-chiseled crowd in Speedos lounges in the afternoon sun.

The beach, of course, is central to the Tel Aviv ideal. Chaise longues line the sand, and masseuses set up shop under umbrellas as halter-topped waitresses bring snacks and drinks. North along the promenade, the rehabilitated old port district is abuzz with restaurants like the open-air Shalvata, where crowds gather on weekends under an expansive canopy of woven palm fronds. Blink and you might as well be in Santa Monica. Mere escapism, or a hymn to life? In the words of one local, it's these simple pleasures—"a good cup of coffee, a day at the beach"— that define happiness in Tel Aviv. +

For The Guide, see page 279.

DAMASCUS

Lost and found
in the Old City

Mannequins sporting hijabs near the Souq al-Hamadiyeh, above. Opposite: Umayyad Mosque.

YIELDING TO DISORIENTATION IN THE MAZE-LIKE CHAOS that is old Damascus is an adventure in itself. The Syrian capital, whose history can be traced back to biblical times, has more to offer than stunning architecture and well-worn relics. Around every one of its dusty corners, discoveries await.

One good place to start is the Souq al-Hamadiyeh, an intoxicating jumble of every Middle Eastern stereotype imaginable: veiled women, piles of spices, horse-drawn carts, mountains of dried figs and nougat. Locals haggle for daily staples such as coffee, rice, and lentils, as shafts of light burst through holes punched in the old iron roof by French machine gunners in the 1920's. From a smoldering wood-fire oven near the ancient Bab Touma gate, a baker retrieves an assortment of *muaarjanat* (filled or flavored breads) topped with tangy *za'atar*, stuffed with white cheese, or slathered with a piquant meaty sauce. At Al-Kamal, freshly squeezed pomegranate juice is served in brimful glasses, along with garlicky *shish touk* (chicken kebabs) and *makdous* (cold, walnut-stuffed eggplant). Arabic coffee infuses the air with the scent of cardamom.

In al-Midan, an ultraconservative part of the city with a jaw-dropping food scene, vendors offer tastes of cheeses, sweeter-than-sweet halvah, and *atayef*—small yeasted pancakes doused in syrup, adorned with *kaymak* (a rich substance made from water buffalo milk), and sprinkled with chopped pistachios. For an archetypal Damascene dessert, navigate the throngs on the main thoroughfare

Chicken kebabs, a Damascus favorite, above. Opposite, clockwise from top left: Coffee beans in the souk; *za'atar* flatbreads, a popular street snack; metalware for sale; a tamarind juice vendor.

Sharia al-Qaimariyya back to the Souq al-Hamadiyeh, where Bekdach has been making ice cream since 1885. The house specialty is *bouza*, an iced confection that's oddly stretchy thanks to the addition of *sahleb*, a starch made from a type of orchid root.

Of course, the city's weighty history and monumental architecture are impossible to ignore. Landmark buildings like the Umayyad Mosque, one of the holiest in all of Islam, began life as a pre-Roman temple over 3,000 years ago. Then there's the old Beit Farhi, a vast residence built by wealthy Spanish Jews; it's currently being restored and will reopen as a boutique hotel. At the Hammam Bakry bathhouse, the Ottoman interior looks like an Ingres painting sprung to life. With sights like this, you'd be hard-pressed to leave Damascus for other destinations in Syria—or even bring yourself to venture past the Old City walls. +

For The Guide, see page 279.

Overlooking the business center of Saigon (Ho Chih Minh City).

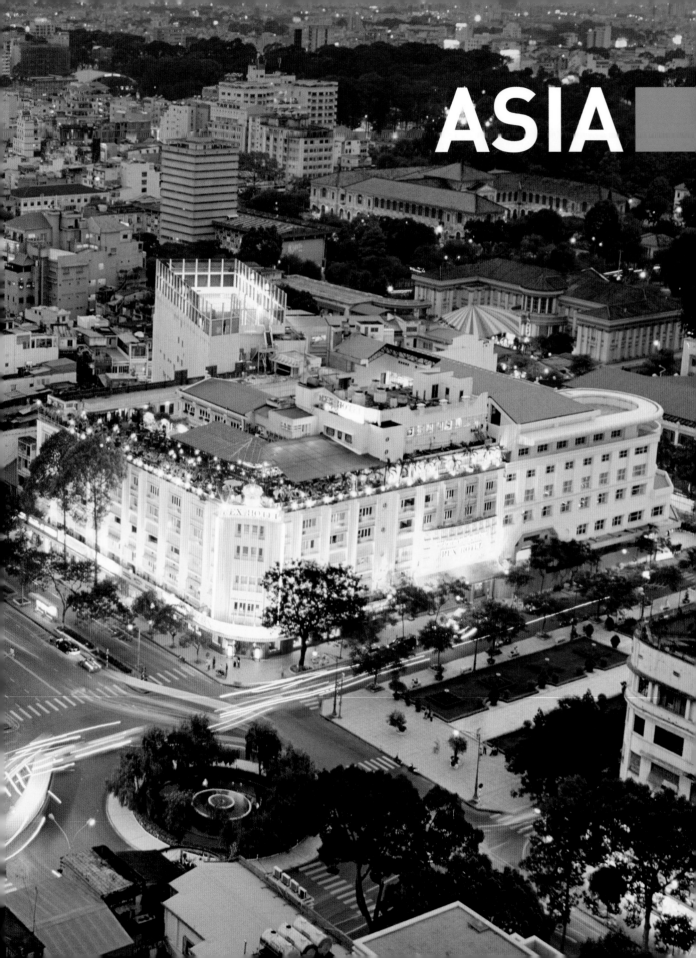

TOKYO

Tasting the city's latest obsessions

THE CAPITAL OF JAPAN may just be the most food-crazed town on earth. Whether it's *kaiten* sushi or *kanten* jelly, cone pizza or collagen-packed soft-shell-turtle meat, this city devours it all. The sublime meets the ridiculous, and handmade collides with high-tech—sometimes all in one bite. Case in point: Gyoza Stadium, a riotous, kitschy sprawl inside the multi-attraction theme-park extravaganza called Namja Town. Faux-rustic booths hawk multicolored gyoza and fat Okinawan pork dumplings; upstairs at Ice Cream City, the 300-some varieties include eel (which has a salty-sweet teriyaki kick and a dusting of *sansho* pepper), and dainty tubs of pearl ice cream in which customers might chance upon a real pearl.

Seventy kinds of salt are on offer at the basement food hall of Takashimaya Times Square, a teeming cathedral of food commerce. On the other end of the spectrum, *konbini* (convenience stores) are Tokyo's shrines to consumerism, with

At the patisserie Sadaharu Aoki, left.
Below: Chirashi-zushi, with shrimp,
salmon roe, cucumber, and lotus root.
Opposite: Namjatown's Ice Cream City.

racks of Kit Kats in limited-edition novelty flavors—cherry blossom, green tea, "chocolatier wine." The sweet-obsessed will be all too happy to join in Japan's pastry-crazed urges. At the Marunouchi salon of idol-pâtissier Sadaharu Aoki, the slender éclairs are almost too beautiful to eat. At Patisserie Satsuki, the *mont blanc* degustation includes a Milano (Italian chestnuts, ricotta, Gorgonzola crust); a Tokyo (Japanese chestnuts and sticky-rice sponge cake); and a Paris (*marron glacé* over a meringue base).

As for savory eats, the prized Ibérico swine is consumed in Japan with such gusto you might wonder if there are any of the acorn-munching black hogs left in Andalusia. The idea of Ibérico pork turned *tonkatsu*—as in proletarian panko-breaded fried pork cutlet—might offend Spanish snobs, but just let those snobs taste it at Butagumi. Literally translated as "pig gang," this new-wave *tonkatsu* temple occupies a quaint timber-framed house in a quiet residential enclave near big, bright Roppongi.

Tachinomiya, standing-room-only bars, have evolved from dives filled with boozy businessmen to sleek watering holes serving Austrian Grüner Veltliner or artisanal sake. Buri, in Ebisu, has an entire wall of color-coordinated miniature sake containers behind its handsome bar. The "one-cup sake" trend—single servings sold in colorful little jars— even inspired a lingerie company to create bras shaped like these miniature vessels. Only in Tokyo, indeed. +

For The Guide, see page 280.

SHIZUOKA

Finding Zen in an age-old ryokan

Clockwise from top left: The Katsura River, next to the Arai Ryokan; a traditional breakfast; shoji screens in a guest room. Opposite: A balcony at the ryokan.

RIDING THE BULLET TRAIN out of Tokyo is like traveling through a painted scroll. The Shinkansen zips you to Mishima, where you can catch a smaller train that purrs through beautiful countryside with Mount Fuji as the backdrop. An hour later, you're in the Shizuoka Prefecture, in the Katsura River town of Shuzenji, which is home to the venerable Arai Ryokan—a 137-year-old *onsen*, or spa, built around a natural hot spring.

Some *onsen* are exclusive and insanely expensive, and others are basic. This one—a clutch of wooden buildings that seem almost Modernist in their simplicity—falls somewhere in the middle. Don slippers and a *yukata* (cotton robe) and head for a soak in the springs, set in a garden with a carp pond. At the bathhouse, wash in the traditional manner before getting into the tubs: sit on a stool, douse yourself with hot and cold spring water from wooden buckets, and scrub down with a rough towel.

Dinner is served in your own guest quarters, at a low table with cushions. Each course is presented as a miniature ceremony—tuna sashimi, arranged like a budding flower; freshly ground wasabi; artfully plated fruit and vegetables. After the meal, the attendant unfurls futons and the fluffiest of duvets, and you're lulled to sleep by the sound of the river. ✦

For The Guide, see page 280.

SEOUL

In search of a striving, thriving metropolis

A reading area at Kyobo Bookshop, one of Seoul's sprawling megastores, left. Below left: Kimchi and other garnishes at Solmoemaeul. Opposite: Photo-booth snapshots at the Lotte World mall, in Seoul's Jamsil neighborhood.

THERE ARE FEW VISTAS IN SEOUL that will leave you gaping in wonder. Concrete and cement are what you will see—horizontally, vertically, diagonally, in the sky, underground—while the flashing, impatient neon logos on most public surfaces are a constant reminder of the pace of life. This is a megacity where past and present, tradition and modernity have not merely collided; they've caused a fission reaction. The secret is to let yourself be a part of the never-ending flow of visual data around you.

Hop on Seoul's efficient subway system and head to the Yongsan Electronics Market, also known as Electroland, where a half-dozen buildings house entire stores devoted to GPS navigators, MP3 players, and hyper-advanced super–cell phones. Apgujeong (or Apgu for short), a kind of instant, vertical Beverly Hills, brims with plastic surgery clinics bearing names such as Smallface and Dream. The din is perpetual, and the commerce flows ceaselessly against the human tide. But Korea's history and its attendant tragedies are just a generation and a demilitarized zone away. The War Memorial of Korea features dioramas of life in wartime; their hokey cardboard nature notwithstanding, the exhibit depicts a civilization that came within millimeters of being completely snuffed out.

And then there's the food—one important key to this culture. At Budnamujip restaurant, the specialty is *galbi*, short ribs traditionally seasoned with such flavors as Asian-pear juice, sesame seed, rice wine, sugar, and that Korean mainstay, garlic (the jolt of sweetness from the complex seasoning is perfect). At Solmoemaeul, in the pleasantly artsy and leafy Samcheong-dong area, the emphasis is on royal cuisine: pumpkin soup, silky acorn jelly, and beef that you wrap in tiny radish crêpes and eat with nine toppings, including mushrooms, seaweed, and carrot strips. The exquisite Bar Da is full of locals munching on dried anchovies as "Hotel California" plays on the radio.

Up Mount Namsan, the new Leeum, Samsung Museum of Art has been spearheading Seoul's reputation as an arts destination. The vast campus consists of a fortress-like homage to terra-cotta designed by Mario Botta, a stainless-steel box by Jean Nouvel, and a slender, light-filled structure by Rem Koolhaas. The objects that glow in the darkness are unmistakably the country's treasures. But for a deeper understanding of the national character, go for a hike on one of the nearby mountains, where senior citizens in Gore-Tex lead a relentless charge up the slopes. This vigor and drive—the need to climb higher and higher until the city you've built spreads before you—is what modern-day Seoul is all about. ✦

For The Guide, see page 280.

Inside Leeum, Samsung Museum of Art, left. Below: The beef *galbi* at Budnamujip restaurant. Opposite: The Myeong-dong shopping district.

Lake Wenhai, left. Below: A vantage point above the first bend of the Yangtze River.

YUNNAN

Hiking China's backcountry

ABOUT AN HOUR INTO A TREK UP THE FOOTHILLS of Yulong Xueshan, or Jade Dragon Snow Mountain, the view opens dramatically. To the north, the mythical dome's snow-covered peak is swathed in tendrils of cloud; below lie the city of Lijiang's cobbled streets and crisscrossing canals. This part of northwest Yunnan is home to the Naxi people, who spend their lives in these hills—medicine men collecting roots and herbs, old women bent double under stacks of firewood, immune to the altitude. Home to China's greatest number of plant and animal species, including the rare Asiatic black bear, the region is now attracting environmentalists' attention. Global organizations like the Nature Conservancy are helping locals set up ecotourism projects as a form of sustainable income.

At the rustic Wenhai Ecolodge—a collectively owned, environmentally minded village enterprise—guest rooms have names like Poppy and Rhododendron (in spring, wildflowers fill the surrounding mountains with color). The lodge reflects traditional Naxi architecture: a walled compound with a central courtyard bordered by timbered wings. Villagers prepare simple, stir-fried fare for guests, as well as *baba*, a Naxi breakfast staple—dough steamed in snowy folds or fried in a wok till golden, served with honey and a hard-boiled egg.

A few hours' drive brings you to Yulong Liming-Laojunshan National Geopark and the serene Lashi Lake, where in winter tens of thousands of migratory birds descend. En route, stop in the town of Shigu to view the famous first bend of the Yangtze River. Wander through the town's chaotic market, bereft of tacky souvenirs and devoted only to life's necessities. You're deep in rural China—with hardly another Westerner to be seen. ✛

For The Guide, see page 280.

LHASA

Tracking change in Tibet

THE WORLD'S HIGHEST RAILWAY connects Beijing to Lhasa—
a controversial line that cost $5 billion and entailed laying
miles of track across fragile tundra. On board, the purpose-
built carriages are fitted with oxygen outlets, special lighting
conductors, and UV-shielded windows. The Chinese
government says the train will be an economic bonanza for
Tibet; critics say it will speed up Chinese settlement and snuff
out Tibetan culture. Undeniably, the journey is an epic one.

Zooming across the tundra
from Lhasa to Beijing.

Pilgrims at Jokhang Temple, below.
Right: Inside the train. Opposite: The
square in front of Jokhang Temple.

The route passes Xi'an, site of China's capital during the Tang Dynasty, and Golmud, located more than 9,000 feet above sea level. (At the station, platform vendors sell giant cucumbers, said to be good for altitude sickness.) The highest point in the journey is Tibet's Tanggula Pass, where mossy tundra sweeps away to distant snowy hills.

A crash of celebratory music greets travelers arriving at the huge Lhasa station, an architectural echo of the monumental Potala Palace across the river. Visits to the palace itself—the former seat of the Tibetan government and residence of past Dalai Lamas—must be prebooked; under new rules, tourists have an hour to get through the colossal site. Even at this pace, it's an unforgettable experience. In each chapel, banks of niches house ancient texts bundled in yellow cloth. The tomb of the "Great Fifth" Dalai Lama is decorated with brocade hangings, gold leaf, and precious stones. All too soon, the tour is over: fourteen centuries of history in a mere 60 minutes.

"Go to the Jokhang Temple at sunrise" is one artist's advice on where to find Tibet's spiritual heart. The temple is the most sacred building in Tibetan Buddhism; prostrating worshippers cluster at the entrance, while an immense queue of pilgrims winds into the dark interior. In the past, people would walk for weeks or months to reach this spot. Today, the journey is easier, but many still do it on foot, some even prostrating themselves every step of the way. The stream of humanity—old women in patterned tunics, kids in Nikes, and tribal Khampa men—is both awe-inspiring and humbling. From the incense stoves, smoke carries the pilgrims' prayers toward the distant hills. +

For The Guide, see page 281.

Businessman Hawkins Pham in Phu My Hung,
left. Above: An apartment complex in Phu My
Hung. Opposite: Stylish local Jap Hoang.

SAIGON

A mad dash to the future

FOR A GLIMPSE OF WHAT ASIA MIGHT BECOME in 10 or 20 years,
there's no place quite like Vietnam—and nowhere as vibrant
as Ho Chi Minh City, the nation's roaring economic engine
and fast-beating heart. The city, still called Saigon by its
8 million residents, is writing a whole new chapter in its long
and dramatic history, and the energy on the streets is palpable.

Once among Asia's poorest nations, Vietnam is quickly
becoming a middle-income country: high-end boutiques
and restaurants no longer cater only to tourists but to trend-
conscious, status-hungry locals. Global influences abound.
The younger generation (three-quarters of the population was
born after 1975) has made a huge
mark, putting a contemporary spin
on Vietnamese classics, from fashion
and design to food. The aptly named
shop Saigon Kitsch trades in Socialist-
themed ephemera—Uncle Ho coffee
mugs, Communist Party T-shirts—
while the Dogma gallery sells vintage
Vietnamese propaganda posters. For
a refined take on traditional street
food, hit the breezy courtyard at Quan
An Ngon for *muc nuong*, a dish of
grilled squid with chili sauce. Or visit
Xu, a trendy restaurant and lounge
specializing in spicy noodle soup,
served up with a side order of

Street fashion as seen on local designer Nha Tanh, above left. Right: Spicy *bun bo Hue* soup at Xu.
Opposite: A billboard for Saigon's new development.

dance-pop. Don't miss a stroll along Ton That Thiep Street, three tree-shaded blocks of colonial-era shop-houses, many now occupied by cool boutiques. It's where you'll also find the Temple Club restaurant, for top-notch Vietnamese food in a retro setting—all polished lacquer, palisander, and opium-den screens.

If you've come to soak up the past, there's still much to see—for now. Saigon's architectural legacy is remarkably diverse: century-old pagodas and squat Chinese godowns abut Art Deco cafés and Modernist apartment blocks. And of course there are the majestic palaces and villas built by the French that earned Saigon the sobriquet "the Paris of the East."

But for a look at that bright gleaming future (or one possible version of it), take a 20-minute taxi ride from downtown Saigon to Phu My Hung. Seven years ago, PMH was mostly bogs and fishing villages. Now it's an ultramodern suburb, complete with lawn sprinklers, speed bumps, and man-made lakes. The broad boulevards are lined with fitness clubs and fast-food chains, backed by glossy condominium towers. Still, even here the past endures: at the edge of one development runs a moss-green river, where fishermen in conical hats paddle in dugout canoes, dragging their nets silently across the water. ✛

For The Guide, see page 281.

PALAWAN

Islands unlimited

ON THIS STRING-BEAN ARCHIPELAGO, resorts linger in splendid isolation, and gorgeous beaches fringe idyllic emerald lagoons. Palawan, one of Asia's last frontiers, is a slender finger that extends south from the rest of the Philippines almost to the tip of Borneo, laying claim to 1,780-plus islands and 1,200 miles of beaches—some so secluded that they've developed a thin, crème brûlée–like crust that breaks only when you set foot on the sand. The sea that surrounds them, home to a stunning array of marine life, encompasses seemingly every gradation of blue in nature's palette.

The fishing village of El Nido serves as Palawan's tourist

All tanked up and ready to dive. Right, from top: Bacuit Bay; a Miniloc lagoon. Opposite: A lazy day on the beach.

center, home to a handful of operators who will find you a boat, jeep, or plane to navigate the region. Hike through the lush green forest to a wooden lookout with a 360-degree view of the seascape: dozens of isles, formed by jagged 250-million-year-old limestone, punch out of the bay into the sky like giant misshapen molars.

On Dilumacad, the sweeping beach is covered in so many shells, it's as if someone came out at dawn every day to spread them underfoot. Nearby Cadlao is a mysterious landmass encircled by reefs—a diver's paradise. A similarly rich underwater world can be found around Miniloc, where parrot fish and clown fish dart among the brain coral. On the far side of Bacuit Bay, Mantiloc has a hole in the limestone wall at low tide, through which snorkelers can enter a shallow lagoon rich in coral—a natural tropical aquarium. Here in Palawan, it's all too easy to lose count of how many beaches and islands you visit; but you'd happily backtrack to get it right. +

For The Guide, see page 281.

BALI

Two sides to a timeless island

A rice paddy field near the town of Ubud, left. Below: Offerings during a temple ceremony. Opposite: A procession at Pura Besakih.

THE LUSH GREEN LANDSCAPE, the volcanoes and the monkey forests, the sparkling rivers and terraced rice paddies: this is Bali. The dreadlocked boys in drum circles, DJs blending electro-funk on MacBooks, expats nursing cocktails at Ku De Ta: this, too, is Bali. Hold on—which is correct?

They're both accurate, and perhaps only Bali could successfully negotiate those two extremes. The island's culture is built on the precepts of harmony and balance: between light and dark, the spiritual and the material, the traditional and . . . whatever comes next. Bali is changing fast—2008 was its biggest tourism year ever, and investment is flooding in; rice paddies are giving way to luxury hotels, and families are selling their plots to the highest bidder. Amid all this commerce, one can't

help wondering if the culture will be devoured along with the land. Are the traditional arts and rituals still alive and relevant? Is Bali still Bali?

The answer is a resounding yes. Wherever you go, you'll see a ritual in progress: a young woman making an offering on the beach by setting afloat a *canang*, a banana-leaf prayer basket full of flowers, incense, and rice. A cremation parade complete with floats and a gamelan orchestra. Whole villages of artisans carving wood and

A cremation in Ubud, below. Right: A Balinese dancer in costume. Opposite: Terraced rice paddies near the village of Teglalang.

stone in the manner of their ancestors. Musicians, dancers, mask-makers, and other artists thriving on classic forms, yet in many cases incorporating global influences into their craft—again, the key is finding the balance.

Such rich traditions remain easily accessible thanks to the Balinese, whose warmth and openheartedness is sadly rare in this day and age. At Pura Besakih, the "mother temple," people of all ages still arrive clad in traditional garb, and even the chatty teenagers fall into a hush when the *mangku*, a priest, sprinkles the crowd with holy water. Of course, every culture is only as strong as the dedication of the next generation. "Young people like to copy other ways, other lifestyles," notes Ida Peranda Wahayan Buruan, one of Bali's 1,000 high priests. "We cannot force their interest. But even if they dye their hair red, they are still Balinese. They will come back to the old ways." +

For The Guide, see page 281.

DELHI

The capital of collective ambition

New Delhi's Imperial Hotel, an Art Deco classic, above left. Right: A street in Old Delhi.
Opposite: The platform at the Connaught Place Metro station.

NOT LONG AGO, DELHI CAME OFF as a rather provincial city: the domain of government bureaucrats, where it was hard to find a beer outside of a hotel bar, and where malls and multiplexes had yet to take root. For all its clamor and chaos, India's capital could feel almost . . . sleepy. Travelers, too, often treated the city as a gateway to more exotic points: Jaipur, Goa, the Taj Mahal. Delhi was what happened while you were making other plans.

Which makes its recent transformation all the more astonishing. Economic liberalization, beginning in the 1990's, coaxed thousands of ambitious arrivals to Delhi from all over the world. Today this is India's most thrillingly diverse and cosmopolitan city, with dozens of languages, ethnicities, and coexisting agendas. Home to India's largest mosque, the world's biggest Hindu temple, and, yes, South Asia's most sprawling shopping mall, Delhi is certainly outsize. But it can also disarm you with intimate moments: on the grounds of Humayun's Tomb, where only the flap of pigeon wings breaks the hush; in the trancelike Sufi Qawwali singing at Nizamuddin's Shrine.

Flush with new money, Delhi has been on a serious civic improvement kick, updating infrastructure, expanding highways, and spiffing up monuments. "It's changing so fast, and I must say it's changing for the good," says Manish Arora, one of the city's preeminent fashion designers. The notorious air pollution has been dramatically reduced, after buses, taxis, and auto rickshaws switched to cleaner-burning natural gas. Connaught Place—the central plaza that was the hub of British life during the Raj—is being restored, its famous

At the Bara Gumbad tomb in the Lodi Garden.
Opposite, from left: In Old Delhi's garment
district; fashion designer Manish Arora.

white facades repainted. And Delhi's long-planned Metro system is not only up and running but has become a bona fide tourist attraction. Fifteen years ago, Delhi residents didn't eat out much: restaurants catered mostly to out-of-towners and businessmen. Now a youthful generation of trendsetters is filling glamorous boîtes like Olive Beach and Threesixty°. Better still, you can find a dizzying array of regional Indian cuisines, from Maharashtrian to Bengali.

For a sprawling metropolis of 17 million people, the city is surprisingly green. Whole swaths are given over to gardens, parks, and protected woodlands. In New Delhi, each major thoroughfare is lined with a particular species of tree: tamarinds on Akbar Road, banyans on Willingdon Crescent. Then there's Lodi Garden, one of the world's great urban parks (with thousands of emerald parakeets). Joggers rest on the crumbling steps of 14th-century mausoleums; yogis do sun salutations beside the ponds; vendors proffer glasses of *jal jeera*, a salty limeade with cumin and mint.

As ever, the most enthralling experiences are to be found in Old Delhi—the walled city built by Mughal emperor Shah Jahan in the 17th century. Take an afternoon to stroll Chandni Chowk, Old Delhi's half-mile-long bazaar. The scent of ground spices mingles with the aroma of street-cart chapatis. Bodies leap and pivot to avoid bullock carts and hurtling pedicabs. Stray cows lap at the pavement; kids play cricket on impossibly narrow lanes. The "old" India is still hidden down these alleyways, veiled in smoke from incense and sidewalk grills—carrying on as if the millennium had never arrived. +

For The Guide, see page 281.

Ahilya Fort, as seen from the Narmada River. Opposite, clockwise from top left: Scattered daybeds in one of the fort's corridors; breakfast in the garden; villagers by the fort; a hammock bed in the prince's private apartment.

MAHESHWAR

Princely hospitality on a sacred river

YOU HEAR A LOT OF BIRDSONG IN MAHESHWAR, in the central Indian state of Madhya Pradesh. There's a near-total absence of the ubiquitous din that pervades more populous parts of the country, thanks to Maheshwar's remoteness and its location on the Narmada, one of the seven most sacred rivers in India.

On five acres overlooking the water, the 18th-century Ahilya Fort was restored by the former prince of Indore and converted into a finely appointed 14-room hotel. Once you've checked in, it's tempting to settle into a rhythm of well-accommodated indolence. Your days are spent wandering the sleepy lanes of Maheshwar; visiting weavers at the Rehwa Society, whose gossamer saris are an essential part of an Indian bride's trousseau; stopping into shrines; plying the river in flat-bottomed boats; and gorging on gourmet meals. Raised beds laid out by the prince, who has even written his own cookbook,

provide oak leaf lettuce and sweet red carrots for salads; the breakfast eggs and chicken travel not food miles, but food feet (a hen house stands beside a fort wall, near the path to the swimming pool). On some nights dinner is set up amid the crenellated palisades, outlined by the light of a thousand oil candles. Other nights, you can dine in the courtyard or be ferried to an island. Drinks are served on a terrace in the ramparts, with views of the wine-dark river and the Shiva temples along the shore. ✦

For The Guide, see page 281.

BANGKOK

The white-hot center of cool

Bangkok's Grand
Palace at night.
Opposite: A young
couple at the Siam
Paragon mall.

BANGKOK IS A WHIRLWIND OF CONTRASTS. The Dubai-style opulence of the Siam Paragon mall—where golf carts whiz across oceanic expanses of marble, and a silent Lamborghini dealership sits above a crowded KFC—is as befuddling as the sweltering streets of the city center. ("The more you shop, the more you get," reads one sign plastered to an elevator—a new reality in today's Asia.) Riding the SkyTrain is like being in an air-conditioned

The glass exterior of the Siam Paragon mall.

middle-class cocoon, far from the Technicolor madness down below. The view appears as a jumble of oxidized hovels, clotheslines, and satellite dishes, with a postmodern cityscape seemingly airlifted from Miami's Brickell Avenue. "The Residence. The Lifestyle. The Address," boasts the tagline for one 71-story condominium, and the SkyTrain is certainly part of that fantasy.

In the dusty maze of *sois*, or side streets, that branch off from Siam Square, foodies flock to humble gems like Som Tam Nua, which could be at home in an L.A. strip mall. From raw mango to spicy pork salad, dinner is a fiesta of strong chile and onions, mopped up with servings of sticky rice. The baskets of crisp fried chicken—marinated overnight in fish sauce and pepper—crackle in your mouth, as deadly and glorious as anything the American South has ever produced.

When evening envelops the relentless megalopolis, Southeast Asia's most fabled nightlife emerges. Tapas Room Club, with its friendly vibe, makes a good introduction to the lay of the land. But the place of the

moment is Bed Supperclub, located on yet another *soi* off Sukhumvit Road. Once past the bouncers, you're in a painfully minimalist white barn headed for outer space; true to the club's name, you can lie down on a series of white, oddly comfy beds. The crowd runs the gamut from clubby expats to showy high-society girls. In a city this swathed in spectacle, it's hard to look away.

Not far from the evening throngs, in the serene temple of Wat Suthat, a 26-foot-high Buddha sits snugly within a tall assembly hall, surrounded by murals that depict his life—murals as complex and elaborate as the street life outside the temple walls. A young man prays over a 20-baht note to be deposited into an alms box. Incense from joss sticks wafts over the fans. Tired workingmen nod off to sleep, cross-legged. The aerials of the busy city peek through the windows. Only then do you get a sense of the one element missing from Bangkok's kaleidoscopic swirl: nothingness. ✦

For The Guide, see page 282.

A fishing boat in Khao Sam Roi Yot National Park, left. Below: A deserted surf shack.

PRANBURI

The makings of a world-class resort

THREE HOURS SOUTH OF BANGKOK, this pine tree–lined stretch of coast is free of the wandering masseurs, banana-boat operators, and other interlopers who crowd many of the country's beaches. You're likely to see only the occasional couple strolling along the sand, enjoying uninterrupted views of fishing boats plying the Gulf of Thailand. Seaside shacks dish up flavorful street food, including *som tam* (spicy green-papaya salad) and honey-basted grilled chicken. A few miles inland, pineapple plantations, mangrove forests, and rice fields attract travelers in search of the Thailand of 20 years ago. Just south of town, the limestone hills, calcite-encrusted caves, and wildlife-rich marshes of Khao Sam Roi Yot National Park provide a sampling of the region's more rugged pleasures.

Change is slowly creeping into Pranburi, announced by charmingly idiosyncratic boutique hotels; its alluring novelty and unspoiled character compel many travelers to choose it over the popular resort town of Hua Hin, 30 minutes north. "Hua Hin is becoming a big city with traffic," says clothing designer Yingluck Charoenying, one of the first Bangkok settlers to open a hotel in the area in 1997. Her whimsical 12-room Brassiere Beach (inspired by two domelike islands that sit just offshore) is a garden oasis of cool blue and whitewashed walls. Other properties, including X2 Kui Buri—a compound of low-slung stone-and-wood bungalows designed by Thai architect Duangrit Bunnag—are also raising Pranburi's international profile. Is this Southeast Asia's next great beach resort? Go now and find out. ✦

For The Guide, see page 282.

LANGKAWI

Island at the crossroads

ABOUT 20 YEARS AGO, Langkawi was remote and untrammeled enough to be considered "the Siberia of Malaysia"— albeit far more welcoming. The world's oversight proved to be Langkawi's gain. This cluster of 99 islands off Malaysia's northwest coast (whose name refers to both the archipelago and its largest island) is a relative neophyte when it comes to tourism. Though development

The façade of the Four Seasons Resort.

A folded-leaf offering, below.
Right: Poolside at Bon Ton Resort.

is on the march, the main island remains a nature-lover's paradise, rich in mangrove and tropical rain forests, mountain ranges, and limestone karsts. In recognition of these assets, along with its diverse wildlife (including more than 220 species of birds), Langkawi was designated a UNESCO Geopark— the first in Southeast Asia.

This is a destination that doesn't lack for magnificent beaches, each with its own vibe and a different set of sunseekers. To the southwest is Pantai Cenang, a strip of talcum-white sand with a row of guesthouses and bars tucked amid coconut palms and casuarinas. Jet Skis and motorboats buzz about the bay, and teenagers flock to a beachside food truck called Tsunami Laksa for *asam laksa* (hot-and-sour fish soup with rice noodles). At the northern tip of the island, Tanjung Rhu is a tranquil oasis: two miles of near-deserted silver sand lapped by calm waters.

Back in the early 1990's, it was the Datai—a luxury resort set amid thick rain forest on a sandy, semi-private cove—that first put Langkawi on the high-end island-hopper's map. Other developments have followed since, including the Four Seasons Resort, on a gorgeous 40-acre site near Tanjung Rhu. Word of mouth is spreading; authorities expect visitor arrivals

A long-tailed macaque, common on Langkawi, below. Left: Inside a villa at Bon Ton Resort.

to increase significantly. Still, much of Langkawi retains its traditional charm, on view at Bon Ton Resort—a small village of formerly dilapidated Malay wooden houses transformed into stylish lodgings by hotelier Narelle McMurtrie. Besides creature comforts like wooden soaking tubs, Bon Ton represents one of the best efforts at cultural preservation on Langkawi.

As ever, the island's greatest thrills derive from exploring its wild side. The infectiously enthusiastic naturalists at the Four Seasons offer guided boat tours of the mangrove forests around the Kilim and Setul karsts; in the labyrinth of waterways, you might spot macaques, huge monitor lizards, mudskippers (fish that emerge from the water to "walk" and feed on land), perhaps even a majestic white-bellied sea eagle. Don't miss a

nature walk with Irshad Mobarak, a big bear of a man with the charisma of a true believer and an encyclopedic knowledge of the rain forest. Mobarak leads early morning treks at the Datai, during which he'll point out saucer-eyed flying lemurs, a variety of wild ginger proven to help prevent stomach cancer, and a red speck on a tree that turns out to be Langkawi's smallest bird. Blink and you might miss it—like this singular island itself. ✦

For The Guide, see page 282.

Overwater bungalows
at the Four Seasons
Resort Bora Bora.

AUSTRALIA+ NEW ZEALAND +THE SOUTH PACIFIC

MELBOURNE

Raising the culinary stakes

Spaghetti *arrabbiatta* in parchment paper at Giuseppe, Arnaldo & Sons, below. Right: The restaurant's namesakes (and owners' fathers). Opposite: The dining room of Bistro Guillaume.

CAN FINE DINING BE AS BIG A DRAW AS gaming? Crown Casino is willing to bet on it. Taking a cue from Las Vegas—a gambling playground turned culinary epicenter—Australia's largest casino complex, on the banks of Melbourne's Yarra River, has also lured a slew of top restaurateurs in a bid to become a serious food destination.

At Bistro Guillaume, rugby-loving chef Guillaume Brahimi, who trained under Joël Robuchon, turns out creative interpretations of French staples like duck confit and *gratin dauphinois*. Don't miss Brahimi's deluxe spin on fish-and-chips: a whole deboned whiting served on potatoes cooked in goose fat. The dining room is a mix of the understated (crisp linen–covered tables) and the fanciful (lampshades that look like dancers' petticoats at Les Folies Bergère).

Seductive Italian fare is the specialty at Giuseppe, Arnaldo & Sons, a charming trattoria named for the owners' fathers. Every dish shimmers with flavor, from the plump *arancini* to the pleasantly bitter *puntarella* salad of chicory, dandelion, anchovy, and asiago. In keeping with the informal atmosphere, house wines are available by the carafe; the glass salumi case is backlit, making the hanging meats glow like a cathedral pietà.

A second home for the expense-account set, Rockpool Bar & Grill pairs a setting of dark leather and timbered woods with a menu featuring a dozen cuts of beef. If you're a steak buff, this is the place to test your mettle. Rounding out the offerings: seafood dishes, sides like onion rings and macaroni and cheese, and a credible vegetable *tagine*. The leather-bound wine list will put even a high roller's wallet to the test. +

For The Guide, see page 282.

NEW SOUTH WALES

The coast less traveled

PRISTINE BEACHES, EXCELLENT DINING, even a kangaroo or two: a seaside jaunt south of Sydney is full of hits. Hop on the Grand Pacific Drive just outside the city, past old coal-mining towns, and you'll soon arrive at the Nan Tien Temple—an enormous Buddhist structure, the kind you always thought you'd need to visit China to see. But there you are, in front of an eight-story pagoda in Australia's New South Wales.

Clockwise from top left: Hyams Beach; leaving Sydney along the Sea Cliff Bridge; bouillabaisse at Berry Sourdough Bakery & Café; a tent at Paperbark Camp. Opposite: Bannisters Point Lodge, on the coast of New South Wales.

Thirty minutes south in the pleasantly quaint town of Berry, the Berry Sourdough Bakery & Café serves a small but ambitious menu, including smoked sardines and twice-cooked pork belly. At Bannisters Point Lodge, a motel recast as a stylish resort, the rooms are all white and wicker, with wooden decks that overlook the Pacific. The next morning, head for Murramarang National Park to check out the resident kangaroos—less the cuddly cartoon animals they're made out to be, unfortunately, than large wild beasts with the scowl of a nightclub bouncer and the hindquarters of a mule.

The inland loop from Mollymook to Huskisson is a 90-minute detour to another world, an Australia that has hardly changed in a millennia. Nearby Hyams Beach is famous for having the world's whitest sand: it's platinum-blonde, bridal-gown pure, a wide-open arc of water and shore. Paperbark Camp, just north of Huskisson, has an entirely different feel. Guests nestle in the woods in solar-powered luxury tents—some have king-size beds and soaking tubs—and sleep zipped up tight against mosquitoes. Leave after breakfast for the 115-mile drive back to Sydney, and you could be lunching at Bondi Beach by early afternoon. +

For The Guide, see page 282.

FAR NORTH QUEENSLAND

Digging into the regional bounty

NO, THE SURF-AND-TURF DIVES and bush food–themed tourist joints haven't been replaced by haute cafés. But a serious culinary movement is under way in Far North Queensland, and the emphasis is increasingly local. This is a food region on the rise—a combination of creative farmers and savvy transplants from Sydney leading a gentle gastronomic boom.

Boats docked at
Cairns Marina.

Outside Nu Nu restaurant, above. Right, from top: Watching out for the locals; *barramundi* with banana bell, a celebration of regional ingredients.

At Twelve Bar Café in Cairns, breakfast consists of "happy eggs" from a free-range poultry farm, plus luscious yogurt and cheeses from a biodynamic dairy in the Cairns hinterland. Going to Rusty's Market is like entering a wonderland of tropical produce: stalls are piled with a blinding jumble of brilliantly colored fruit, including ruby-red lychees, hairy rambutans, flamboyant dragon fruit, and spiky durian. To go straight to the source, head to the fertile Atherton Tablelands, a dense green plateau that's ideal for growing everything from bamboo shoots to grass for dairy cows. The coffee industry has been alive and well in this part of the world for several decades; Skybury and Coffee Works, two of the larger plantations in the Mareeba region, offer tours and tastings.

Back in Cairns, the Vannella Cheese Factory sells a legendary *bufalina*, a tiny buffalo mozzarella made by owner Vito Minoia and his son Giuseppe. Try it atop the pizza at Piccolo Cucina, or in the reinvented "caprese" at Nu Nu, where chef Nick Holloway pairs the cheese with juicy persimmon garnished with sage and walnuts. It's fresh, creative, and delicious—an apt embodiment of the region's culinary ambitions. +

For The Guide, see page 282.

THE TOP END

Legends of the outback

A safari bungalow at the
Bamurru Plains bush camp,
in northern Australia.

EVEN THE CROWS sound different here. Their strangled clacking has a higher timbre and a more staccato rhythm than that of their larger cousins in the Northern Hemisphere. But the birds are just one of many elements that make this stretch of Australia seem straight out of a fairy tale. The Top End encompasses some of the world's least populated, most climatically diverse regions, from saltwater estuaries and arid savanna to hidden thermal springs and impassable peaks—landscapes made famous by Baz Luhrmann's 2008 film epic, *Australia*.

Aboriginal children preparing for a ceremonial performance, below. Right: The Bungle Bungle rock formations in Purnululu National Park.

The still-flourishing ancient narrative traditions add to the otherworldly draw. In Aboriginal Dreamtime myths, totemic ancestors traveled the landscape, scattering a trail of musical notes that serve as geological markers. Trees, rocks, creeks, patches of desert, whole mountain ranges—even diminutive dust storms called willy-willys—are part of the "song lines." Every creature is connected to a specific aspect of this sacred geography by a "Dreaming" story and a bloodline.

Trekking on your own? Start at Warmun Roadhouse, a dusty pit stop on the Great Northern Highway. Like many of its kind along the Top End's barren roads, this is a gathering point where travelers can find food, fuel, and basic bed-and-shower facilities. Just outside town, Purnululu National Park is a UNESCO World Heritage site that encompasses the Bungle Bungle Range—20 million–year–old striped rock formations that resemble giant beehives. The typical Aboriginal art palette is based on the natural tinctures available regionally, such as ground ocher and white clay, and Top End artists are considered some of Australia's most creative. In the mining and cattle town of Kununurra, you can see painters in action at the Waringarri Aboriginal Arts studio.

Beyond Kununurra lie the East Kimberley plains, fenced in by sprawling cattle stations. A cluster of boab trees and a new stone wall mark the entrance to Home Valley Station, a 615,000-acre parcel held in trust for Aboriginal landholders. From here, a day's drive northeast will land you at the Mary River floodplain, on the doorstep of Kakadu National Park; settle in at the eco-conscious bush camp Bamurru Plains, which has a collection of modern Aboriginal art and an open-air bar of coveted Australian wines. Feast on rack of lamb and wattleseed cheesecake by the light of a kerosene lamp, then collapse onto your platform bed and listen to wallabies hop around in the brush outside. +

For The Guide, see page 283.

SOUTHLAND

New Zealand's next big thing?

FEW NEW ZEALANDERS—AND EVEN FEWER foreigners, for that matter—venture south beyond iconic Milford Sound or adventure outfitter–packed Queenstown. Yet this sparsely populated natural wonderland is full of under-visited attractions: pristine forests, waterfalls, lakes, and spectacular stretches of coast. Southland is being touted as a destination in the making, but its remoteness ensures it will stay off the beaten track for quite some time.

At Te Anau, a two-hour drive from Queenstown, the Fiordland Lodge makes the perfect overnight base for visiting the country's most dramatic fjords—Milford and the less famous Doubtful Sound. An hour and 15 minutes south, the straw-bale Tikana Lodge is located on a secluded 100-acre farm in Winton, surrounded by paddocks with grazing deer. On a clear day, owners Donna-Maree Day and Dave Lawrence will guide you to the top of a hill to see the outline of Stewart Island, the country's third biggest landmass. In the Catlins, where rugged coast fronts dense rain forest, stop at the beaches of Curio Bay—and don't miss the petrified fossil forest, where 160-million-year-old logs stand frozen in time at the water's edge. Get back in touch with civilization in the university town of Dunedin, where the Mandeno House bed-and-breakfast serves tea in a formal rose garden. +

For The Guide, see page 283.

Fiordland Lodge at Te Anau.
Opposite: Pura Kaunui Falls
one of Southland's
natural wonders.

BORA-BORA

Living the barefoot life

A bird's-eye view of Bora-Bora, left. Below: An overwater bungalow at Four Seasons Resort Bora Bora. Opposite: The Four Seasons' white-sand beach.

BARRIER REEFS MEET COBALT LAGOONS; volcanic peaks rise above tropical rain forest and powder-soft beaches. This South Pacific idyll is the quintessential far-flung escape, but fortunately it's no longer all that difficult to get to—a nonstop flight from Los Angeles will swoop you here in just over eight hours.

Romance comes easy on Bora-Bora, a textbook honeymooners' paradise. The recently opened Four Seasons Resort Bora Bora has 121 thatched-roof bungalows set on piers over the shallows, with deep-soaking tubs that have views of the lagoon. You can take a half-day sail to hidden snorkeling sites, visit a black-pearl farm, or spend an afternoon doing nothing more than lounging indolently on the deck of a catamaran. More affordable accommodations can be found at the 80-room Novotel Bora Bora Beach Resort, a Polynesian-style retreat with kayaks, jet skis, and snorkeling gear at the ready. Nearby, you'll find the five-table restaurant Villa Mahana, where Corsican-born chef Damian Rinaldi Dovio reinvents native ingredients (Tahitian vanilla, coconut milk) with classic French techniques. Order the mahimahi in a curried banana crust or the seared tuna with vanilla oil; and finish with the mango sorbet, freshly churned from local fruits. +

For The Guide, see page 283.

THE MARQUESAS ISLANDS

Solitude by the sea

THE THREE-HOUR FLIGHT FROM TAHITI OVER THE SOUTHERN PACIFIC, with nothing below but whitecaps, only serves to remind you just how distant the Marquesas are from everywhere else. This archipelago, an outpost of French Polynesia, has the geographic distinction of being the farthest group of islands from any continental landmass. The main island of Hiva Oa lacks the blue lagoons and overwater bungalows of Bora-Bora, but travelers in search of peace and quiet will find it here in the primeval landscape of cliffs, waterfalls, and forests.

The sole hotel, Hiva Oa Hanakee Pearl Lodge, has 14 bamboo-lattice accommodations outfitted with woven-palm wall coverings, carved tiki poles, and traditional bark-paper paintings. Arrange an island tour with Pearl Lodge guide Tematai Lecortier, who will point out trellised vanilla orchids and petroglyphs while expertly maneuvering dirt-road switchbacks under a canopy of acacia and mango trees. He'll drive you by Polynesia's largest stone tiki before stopping for a typical Marquesan lunch (which might include tuna ceviche, goat curry, and fried breadfruit) at the house of native chef Pua Poevai.

In the main village, Atuona, the narrow thoroughfare is lined with shops selling Tahitian beer and one-story houses with fishing boats in their yards. Pay your respects at the grave of French artist Paul Gauguin (who spent his final years on the island) at the village's Calvary Cemetery, and view reproductions of his works at the Paul Gauguin Cultural Center. End the day with a stroll on the black sand beach at the base of 4,186-foot Mount Temetiu, secure in the knowledge that very few travelers have done the same.

For The Guide, see page 283.

The pool at Hiva Oa Hanakee Pearl Lodge. Opposite: The Church of Vaitahu, on Tahuata Island in the Marquesas.

→ THE GUIDE

UNITED STATES + CANADA

MAINE

WHERE TO STAY

Captain Lord Mansion
Pale yellow 1812 folly
with Federal-era
antiques and stately
fireplaces. 6 Pleasant St.,
Kennebunkport; 800/522-
3141 or 207/967-3141;
captainlord.com;
doubles from **$$**.

Hidden Pond Two-bedroom
cottages with kitchens,
screened porches, and
outdoor showers on 60
wooded acres. Breakfast
arrives by golf cart.
354 Goose Rocks Rd.,
Kennebunkport; 888/967-
9050; hiddenpondmaine.
com; doubles from **$$$**.

WHERE TO EAT

Blue Sky Sleek, modern
outpost from celebrated
Boston chef Lydia Shire. The
menu includes her famous
lobster pizza (way better
than it sounds). 2 Beach St.,
York Beach; 207/363-0050;
dinner for two ⟟⟟⟟.

**Chauncey Creek Lobster
Pier** Choose your catch
from the tank and enjoy
it on a riverside picnic
table; BYO everything else.
16 Chauncey Creek Rd.,
Kittery Point; 207/439-1030;
lobsters market price.

MC Perkins Cove Knockout
ocean views; plank-roasted
cod and deconstructed clam

chowder. 111 Perkins Cove
Rd., Ogunquit; 207/646-
6263; dinner for two ⟟⟟⟟.

WHAT TO SEE & DO

Fort Foster Town park with
88 acres and the remains of
a circa-1910 naval bunker.
Pocahontas Rd., Kittery
Point; 207/439-3800.

Nubble Light Iconic
lighthouse on rocky
headlands near the York
River. Nubble Rd., Cape
Neddick; lighthouse.cc/
capeneddick.

CAPE COD, MA

WHERE TO STAY

Chatham Bars Inn Cape
Cod's original luxury
hotel, on the waterfront.
297 Shore Rd., Chatham;
800/527-4884 or 508/945-
0096; chathambarsinn.com;
doubles from **$**.

Whalewalk Inn & Spa
Sixteen antiques-filled
rooms and suites in an
1830 main house and
five cottages. 220 Bridge
Rd., Eastham; 800/440-
1281 or 508/255-0617;
whalewalkinn.com;
doubles from **$**.

WHERE TO EAT

**Cap't Cass Rock Harbor
Seafood** Funky shack
serving up no-nonsense
Cape Cod classics. Hours
are strict—11 a.m. to 2 p.m.
for lunch, 5 p.m. to 8 p.m.
for dinner. 117 Rock Harbor
Rd., Orleans; no phone;
lunch for two ⟟⟟.

Lobster Pot Order it
steamed, with drawn

Alaska

Seattle

Idaho   Stillwater

Napa
Valley

Utah
+ Nevada

Aspen

Niagara
Falls

Montreal

Maine
Cape Cod
Block Isla

Upper Peninsula

New York City
New Jersey

Tucson

Asheville

Los Angeles

New Mexico

Memphis

New
Orleans

Milford
Hudson River Valley

Virginia

Palm Beach

Waikiki   Hawaii

**UNITED STATES
+
CANADA**

butter, at this restaurant
on the town's main drag.
321 Commercial St.,
Provincetown; 508/487-
0842; dinner for two ⟟⟟.

Wicked Oyster One of the
best seafood spots on the
Cape. 50 Main St., Wellfleet;
508/349-3455; dinner
for two ⟟⟟.

WHERE TO SHOP

Briar Lane Jams & Jellies
Almost 50 varieties of
cane sugar–sweetened
preserves, in an open-air
stand along the highway.
Rte. 6 and Briar Lane,
Wellfeet; 561/762-6911.

Periwinkle Brightly colored
wares for the home.
25 Bank St., Wellfeet;
561/762-6911.

The Shell Shop The place
for a kitschy seashell-
encrusted souvenir.
276 rear Commercial St.,
Provincetown; 508/
487-1763.

Weekend The Cape's
sleekest boutique,
with goods that range
from clothing to home
acccessories. 217 Main St.,
Orleans; 508/255-9300.

BLOCK ISLAND, RI

WHERE TO STAY

Atwood Real Estate Wide
range of houses for rent.
Chapel St.; 401/466-5582;
weekly rentals from **$$$$**.

Hotel Manisses Quaint
rooms outfitted with

Victorian furnishings in a 138-year-old hotel. 1 Spring St., 401/466-2421; doubles from **$$**.

WHERE TO EAT

Eli's Restaurant Twelve tables and a buzzy bar; local seafood dishes are the specialties. 456 Chapel St., 401/466-5230; dinner for two ❙❙.

Oar Restaurant Lobster rolls, frozen drinks, and a good view of the harbor. 221 Jobs Hill Rd.; 401/466-8820; dinner for two ❙.

Three Sisters Creatively named sandwiches in a faded-wood bungalow near Mansion Beach. Old Town Rd.; 401/466-9661; lunch for two ❙.

WHAT TO SEE & DO

Aldo's Mopeds and Bikes Wheels for rent. Weldon Way; 401/466-5018.

HUDSON RIVER VALLEY, NY

WHERE TO STAY

Madalin Hotel Eleven rooms mix old and new, as in flat-screen TV's atop antique bureaus. 53 Broadway, Tivoli; 845/757-2100; madalinhotel.com; doubles from **$$**.

Rhinecliff Hotel Renovated 1854 property that's once again a bustling hub. Most of the rooms have balconies that seem to float over the Hudson. 4 Grinnell St., Rhinecliff; 845/876-0590; therhinecliff.com; doubles from **$$**.

WHERE TO EAT

DABA Hudson's most ambitious and innovative restaurant, with Scandinavian culinary leanings. 225 Warren St., Hudson; 518/249-4631; dinner for two ❙❙❙.

Homespun Foods Café and hangout for Beacon's artsy crowd. 232 Main St., Beacon; 845/831-5096.

Mercato Local favorite featuring housemade pappardelle and an adjacent pasta shop. 61 E. Market St., Red Hook; 845/758-5879; dinner for two ❙❙.

Terrapin Red Bistro Choose your own bun, cheese, sauce, and extras to dress the all-natural beef burger. 6426 Montgomery St., Rhinebeck; 845/876-3330; lunch for two ❙❙.

WHAT TO SEE & DO

Dia:Beacon Former Nabisco factory showing monumental modern art, like Richard Serra's 1997 *Torqued Ellipses*. 3 Beekman St., Beacon; 845/440-0100; diabeacon.org.

Fisher Center for the Performing Arts At Bard College, Frank Gehry's iconic structure hosts events as creative as its architecture. Annandale-on-Hudson; 845/758-7900; bard.edu/fishercenter.

WHERE TO SHOP

Hudson City Books Owner Karen Montone lives above her shop of 12,000 tomes (used, vintage, and antique). 553 Warren St.; 518/671-6020.

Paper Trail Whimsical gifts and housewares: birdcages, bookends, ribbons, and hand-blocked quilts from India. 6423 Montgomery St., Rhinebeck; 845/876-8050.

NEW YORK CITY

WHERE TO STAY

Inn at Irving Place Nine bedrooms in two adjoining Victorian town houses, near bustling Union Square. 56 Irving Pl.; 212/533-4600;

innatirving.com; doubles from **$$$**.

Lafayette House East Village pied-à-terre, with antiques and fireplace suites. 38 E. Fourth St.; 212/505-8100; lafayettenyc.com; doubles from **$$$**.

WHERE TO EAT

Café Cluny Neighborhood bistro serving Gallic favorites like *poulet rotî* and *frisée aux lardons*. 284 W. 12th St.; 212/255-6900; dinner for two ❙❙❙.

NIGHTLIFE

Oak Bar Newly reopened hideaway in the venerable Plaza Hotel. Fifth Ave. at Central Park S.; 212/758-7777.

Salon de Ning Rooftop bar at the Peninsula Hotel, with an open-air terrace overlooking Fifth Avenue. 700 Fifth Ave.; 212/247-2200.

Smith & Mills Tiny TriBeCa watering hole in a former carriage house. 71 N. Moore St.; no phone.

NEW JERSEY

WHERE TO STAY

Congress Hall Bright, beachy interiors behind a Federal-style façade. 251 Beach Ave. 888/944-1816 or 609/884-8421; congresshall.com; doubles from **$$**.

Virginia Hotel Restored Victorian with opulent yet airy rooms. 25 Jackson St.; 800/732-4236 or 609/884-5700; virginiahotel.com; doubles from **$$**.

Star Inn Nine rooms and two suites, plus 10 chic motel rooms—with full access to Congress Hall's amenities across the street. 29 Perry St.; 888/944-1816 or 609/884-4590; thestarinn.com; doubles from **$**.

WHERE TO EAT

Ebbitt Room Cape May's top spot for a memorable meal, with service to match. At the Virginia Hotel. 25 Jackson St.; 609/884-5700; dinner for two ❙❙❙.

Lobster House Sought-after seafood served on checkerboard tablecloths on the wharf. Cape May Harbor; 609/884-8296; dinner for two ❙❙❙.

MILFORD, PA

WHERE TO STAY & EAT

Hotel Fauchère Rooms with rain showers, radiant-heat floors, and Frette linens. Chef Michael Glatz oversees the formal Delmonico Room (dinner for two ❙❙❙❙) and the bistro-style Bar Louis (dinner for two ❙❙). 401 Broad St.; 570/409-1212; hotelfauchere.com; doubles from **$**.

Lodge at Woodloch Woodsy spa resort near Milford. 109 River Birch Lane, Hawley; 866/953-8500 or 570/685-8500; thelodgeatwoodloch.com; doubles from **$$$$$**, including meals and activities.

WHAT TO SEE & DO

Grey Towers Richard Morris Hunt–designed turreted mansion at the edge of town. 151 Grey Towers Dr.; 570/296-9630; fs.fed.us/gt; tours daily, 11 a.m. to 4 p.m., Memorial Day through late October.

VIRGINIA

WHERE TO STAY

1804 Inn at Barboursville Vineyards Stately Georgian manor and 18th-century cottage, a short stroll from the picturesque ruins of a

LODGING   under $150 → **$** $150–$299 → **$$** $300–$699 → **$$$** $700–$999 → **$$$$** $1,000 + up → **$$$$$**

Thomas Jefferson–designed house. 17655 Winery Rd., Barboursville; 540/832-5384; barboursvillewine.com; doubles from **$$**.

Inn at Little Washington Extravagant cocoon of Brunschwig & Fils fabrics combined with impeccable service. Middle and Main Sts., Washington, VA; 540/675-3800; theinnat littlewashington.com; doubles from **$$$**.

WHERE TO EAT

Mas Authentic tapas (grilled *gambas*, killer tortilla) from chef Tomas Rahal. 501 Monticello Rd., Charlottesville; 434/979-0990; dinner for two ♀♀.

WHAT TO SEE & DO

Barboursville Vineyards Producer of top-notch Barberas and Sangioveses. 17655 Winery Rd., Barboursville; 540/832-3824; barboursville wine.com.

Mountfair Vineyards Focuses on small-batch, Bordeaux-style blends. 4875 Fox Mountain Rd., Crozet; 434/823-7605; mountfair.com.

White Hall Vineyards Good picnic grounds; bring home the jammy Petit Verdot. 5282 Sugar Ridge Rd., White Hall; 434/823-8615; whitehallvineyards.com.

WHERE TO SHOP

Georgie Fashion-forward boutique in the trendy Warehouse District. 126 Garrett St., Charlottesville; 434/295-5001.

ASHEVILLE, NC

WHERE TO STAY

Black Walnut Bed & Breakfast Elegant 1899 inn with seven rooms and top-notch breakfasts prepared by its owners. 288 Montford Ave.; 800/381-3878 or 828/254-3878; blackwalnut.com; doubles from **$$**.

Grand Bohemian Hotel Asheville The city's newest upscale property, with a gallery featuring works by regional and European artists. 11 Boston Way; 877/274-1242 or 828/505-2949; bohemianasheville.com; doubles from **$$**.

Inn on Biltmore Estate Recently refurbished rooms in grand Biltmore style. 1 Approach Rd.; 800/411-3812 or 828/225-1600; biltmore.com; doubles from **$$**.

WHERE TO EAT

Early Girl Eatery Southern breakfast staples served all day. 8 Wall St.; 828/259-9292; brunch for two ♀.

Table Restaurant Seasonal fare served in a minimalist space. 48 College St.; 828/254-8980; dinner for two ♀♀♀.

WHAT TO SEE & DO

Biltmore Estate Philanthropist George Vanderbilt's former residence, inspired by French Renaissance châteaux. 1 Approach Rd.; 877/245-8667 or 828/225-1333; biltmore.com.

MEMPHIS

WHERE TO STAY

Madison Hotel Boutique property in a former bank building, with jewel-toned colors and portraits of blues artists. 79 Madison Ave.; 866/446-3674 or 901/333-1215; madisonhotel memphis.com; doubles from **$$**.

The Peabody Historic hotel with traditions like afternoon tea and the twice-daily Peabody Duck March. 149 Union Ave.; 901/529-4000; peabodymemphis.com; doubles from **$$**.

WHERE TO EAT

Charlie Vergos' Rendezvous Cavernous maze of dining rooms and a renowned slab of ribs. 52 S. Second St.; 901/523-2746; lunch for two ♀♀.

Cozy Corner Grilled Cornish game hen served with Wonder Bread, and barbecue spaghetti. 745 North Pkwy.; 901/527-9158; lunch for two ♀.

Neely's Bar-B-Que Tavern-like setting; luscious pulled-pork platter. 5700 Mount Moriah Rd., and other locations; 901/795-4177; lunch for two ♀.

Tops Bar-B-Q Local chain that's a primer to the Memphis barbecue scene. 2748 Lamar St., and other locations; 901/743-3480; lunch for two ♀.

PALM BEACH, FL

WHERE TO STAY

The Breakers Palm Beach Italianate resort that's been a society fixture since 1904. 1 S. County Rd.; 888/273-2537 or 561/655-6611; thebreakers.com; doubles from **$$$**.

Four Seasons Resort Palm Beach Elegant respite from downtown, with a new 11,000-square-foot spa. 2800 S. Ocean Blvd.; 800/332-3442 or 561/582-2800; fourseasons.com; doubles from **$$$**.

WHERE TO EAT

Bistro Chez Jean-Pierre The ne plus ultra of chichi Palm Beach exhibitionism. 132 N. County Rd.; 561/833-1171; dinner for two ♀♀♀♀.

La Sirena No-nonsense Mediterranean fare and outstanding desserts. 6316 S. Dixie Hwy., West Palm Beach; 561/585-3128; dinner for two ♀♀♀.

Palm Beach Grill Seafood, steak, and stellar service at this casual standby. 340 Royal Poinciana Way, No. 336; 561/835-1077; dinner for two ♀♀♀.

WHERE TO SHOP

Dolce Antiques South Dixie Highway's most over-the-top emporium. 3700 S. Dixie Hwy., West Palm Beach; 561/832-4550.

Shi & Erhard Eclectic mix of antiques and contemporary furniture, behind an attention-getting façade. 431 Bunker Rd., West Palm Beach; 561/588-7288.

Shi Shi Gallery Fanciful women's clothing and accessories, both vintage and new. 3230 S. Dixie Hwy., West Palm Beach; 561/228-8996.

NEW ORLEANS

WHERE TO STAY

Columns Hotel Mansion with a wide wooden porch perfect for sipping Sazeracs, the city's official cocktail. 3811 St. Charles Ave.; 504/899-9308; thecolumns.com; doubles from **$$**.

La Maison Marigny B&B mixing modern and antique in the Faubourg Marigny district, just beyond the French Quarter. 1421 Bourbon St.; 800/570-2014 or 504/948-3638; lamaisonmarigny.com; doubles from **$**.

WHERE TO EAT

August Noted chef John Besh's award-winning paean to the locavore movement. 301 Tchoupitoulas St.; 504/299-9777; dinner for two ♀♀♀.

DINING   under $25 →♀ $25–$74 →♀♀ $75–$149 →♀♀♀ $150–$299 →♀♀♀♀ $300 + up →♀♀♀♀♀

Casamento's Garden District oyster house; only open in the "r" months. 4330 Magazine St.; 504/895-9761; lunch for two ↑↑.
Cochon Contemporary Cajun. 930 Tchoupitoulas St.; 504/588-2123; dinner for two ↑↑.
Coffea Café Doubles as a gallery space. 3218 Dauphine St.; 504/342-2484; breakfast for two ↑.
Elizabeth's Homey restaurant along the river, known for weekend brunch. 601 Gallier St.; 504/944-9272; breakfast for two ↑↑.
Mother's Classic stop for baked ham since 1938. 401 Poydras St. at Tchoupitoulas; 504/523-9656; breakfast for two ↑.
Parkway Bakery & Tavern Best po'boys in town, on distinctive French bread. 538 Hagan Ave.; 504/482-3047; lunch for two ↑.

THE UPPER PENINSULA, MI

WHERE TO STAY
Landmark Inn Historic 62-room hotel with stained-glass windows and rooms overlooking the lake. 230 N. Front St., Marquette; 888/752-6362 or 906/228-2580; thelandmarkinn.com; doubles from $.
Sand Hills Lighthouse Inn Eight rooms in a converted lighthouse. Five Mile Point Rd., Ahmeek; 906/337-1744; sandhillslighthouseinn.com; doubles from $.
WHERE TO EAT
Amy J's Pasty & Bake Shop Supplier of meat-and-potato pasties, an Upper Peninsula delicacy brought over by Cornish miners. 1000 N. Lincoln Dr., Hancock; 906/482-2253.

The Baraga Drive-In Pure nostalgia: hot dogs, root beer floats, and frozen custards. 1156 Superior Ave., Baraga; 906/353-6202; lunch for two ↑.
Harbor Haus Schnitzels and grilled trout served by dirndl-clad waitresses. 77 Brockway Ave., Copper Harbor; 906/289-4502; dinner for two ↑↑.
WHAT TO SEE & DO
Lakenenland Sculpture park with a path for cars, created by a welder who uses scrap metal to craft his works. 108 Timber Lane, Marquette; 906/249-1132; lakenenland.com.
Quincy Mine Museum and guided tours of the former copper mine. 49750 U.S. Hwy. 41, Hancock; 906/482-3101; quincymine.com.
WHERE TO SHOP
Red Barn Antiques Copper keepsakes and locally made wooden bowls. N7017 Au Train-Forest Lake Rd., Au Train; 906/892-8455.

STILLWATER, MN

WHERE TO STAY
Lowell Inn Restored 1927 hotel with two opulent dining rooms. 102 N. 2nd Street; 888/569-3554 or 651/439-1100; lowellinn.com; doubles from $.
Rivertown Inn Victorian mansion with 19th-century antiques and flowering gardens. 306 W. Olive St.; 651/430-2955; rivertowninn.com; doubles from $.
WHERE TO EAT
Leo's Grill & Malt Shop For a 1950's fix. 131 Main St.; 651/351-3943; lunch for two ↑.
WHERE TO SHOP
Midtown Antique Mall Sixty-five antiques dealers

with wares ranging from Mission-style furniture to 1940's dresses. 301 S. Main St.; 651/430-0808.
Rose Mille Mix of vintage and artist-made housewares, and women's clothing. 125 S. Main St.; 651/439-0205.
Staples Mill Antiques Booths for antiques vendors in a converted sawmill. 410 N. Main St.; 651/430-1816.
St. Croix Antiquarian Booksellers More than 60,000 used, rare, and out-of-print books. 132 S. Main St.; 651/430-0732.

ASPEN, CO

WHERE TO STAY
Aspen Meadows Resort Sprawling property that's home to the venerable Aspen Institute. 845 Meadows Rd.; 800/452-4240; dolce-aspen-hotel.com; doubles from $$$.
Little Nell Iconic luxury hotel at the base of Aspen Mountain. 675 E. Durant Ave.; 888/843-6355 or 970/920-4600; thelittlenell.com; doubles from $$$$.
WHERE TO EAT
Elevation Local favorite serving American fare and açai martinis. 304 E. Hopkins Ave.; 970/544-5166; dinner for two ↑↑↑.
Montagna Artisanal fare that uses ingredients from the chef's own organic farm. At the Little Nell. 675 E. Durant Ave.; 970/920-6330; dinner for two ↑↑↑.
Social Scene-setting new addition to Aspen's restaurant row. 304 E. Hopkins Ave.; 970/925-9700; dinner for two ↑↑↑.
WHERE TO SKI
Aspen Highlands Home to the famed Highland

Bowl. 76 Boomerang Rd.; 800/525-6200; aspensnowmass.com.
Aspen Mountain The first of Aspen's four mountains, and its most centrally located. 601 E. Dean St.; 800/525-6200; aspensnowmass.com.
Snowmass The largest of Aspen/Snowmass's four mountains; site of a buzzworthy new base village. 45 Village Square; 800/525-6200; aspensnowmass.com.

NEW MEXICO

WHERE TO STAY
Los Poblanos Inn & Cultural Center Centuries-old hacienda with seven guest rooms and an organic farm. 4803 Rio Grande N.W., Los Ranchos de Albuquerque; 505/344-9297; lospoblanos.com; doubles from $.
Tamaya Resort and Spa Sprawling Native American–owned hotel near Bernalillo, with golf and plenty of post-adventure pampering. 1300 Tuyuna Trail, Santa Ana Pueblo; 800/233-1234 or 505/867-1234; hyatt.com; doubles from $$.
WHERE TO EAT
Daily Pie Cafe and Pie-O-Neer Two outposts for Pie Town's homegrown specialty. Rte. 60, Pie Town; Daily Pie Café, 575/772-2700; Pie-O-Neer, 575/772-2711; slices from ↑.
Yaaka Café Traditional Acoma dishes, as well as hearty regional favorites like elk burgers and green-chile pork stew. Sky City Cultural Center, Acoma Pueblo; 800/747-0181; lunch for two ↑.

LODGING   under $150 → $ $150–$299 → $$ $300–$699 → $$$ $700–$999 → $$$$ $1,000 + up → $$$$$

WHAT TO SEE & DO
Bosque del Apache National Wildlife Refuge Along the Rio Grande, a picturesque habitat for migratory birds. San Antonio; 575/835-1828.
The Lightning Field Internationally acclaimed art installation requiring an overnight stay. Outside Quemado; 505/898-3336; lightningfield.org; March 1–Oct. 31; admission from $150 per person, including meals and lodging.
Sky City Cultural Center Take a 90-minute guided tour of the ancient, still-vibrant pueblo at the top of the sandstone mesa. Acoma Pueblo; 800/747-0181; acomaskycity.org; tours $20.
Very Large Array Roadside collection of giant satellite dishes, plus fascinating exhibits about life in outer space. 35 miles east of Pie Town on Rte. 60; www.vla.nrao.edu.

TUCSON, AZ

WHERE TO STAY
Arizona Inn Pink adobe-style resort on 14 acres of lush gardens. 2200 E. Elm St.; 800/933-1093 or 520/325-1541; arizonainn.com; doubles from **$$**.
Tanque Verde Ranch Dude ranch with wilderness rides. 14301 E. Speedway Blvd.; 800/234-3833 or 520/296-6275; tanqueverderanch.com; doubles from **$$$**, all-inclusive.
WHERE TO EAT
Café Poca Cosa Regional darling Susana Davila's showcase of nouvelle-Mexican fare. 110 E. Pennington St.; 520/622-6400; dinner for two †††.
Cup Café Stellar breakfast spot inside the laid-back Hotel Congress. 311 E. Congress St.; 520/798-1618; breakfast for two †.
The Dish Bistro and wine bar behind the RumRunner wine shop. 3131 E. First St.; 520/326-1714; dinner for two †††.
Janos Fine-dining restaurant from award-winning chef Janos Wilder. 3770 E. Sunrise Dr.; 520/615-6100; dinner for two †††.
WHAT TO SEE & DO
Mt. Lemmon General Store Local institution with a decadent array of housemade fudge. 12856 N. Sabino Canyon Pkwy.; 520/576-1468.
Saguaro National Park Surprisingly lush desert landscape to the east and west of Tucson. Both areas have excellent hiking trails and scenic drives. nps.gov/sagu.

UTAH + NEVADA

WHERE TO STAY
Flanigan's Inn Compound with a spa, a hilltop labyrinth, and the popular Spotted Dog Café. Zion National Park is a five-minute walk away. 450 Zion Park Blvd., Springdale, Utah; 800/765-7787; discoverzion.com; doubles from **$**.
Red Mountain Resort & Spa Outdoor options abound: yoga or tai chi on the rocks, biking, even a hike with dogs from the local animal shelter. 1275 E. Red Mountain Circle, Ivins, Utah; 877/246-4453; redmountainspa.com; from **$$** per person, including meals and some activities.
Zion Lodge Inside Zion National Park, right across from the Emerald Pools trail. Springdale, Utah; 888/297-2757; doubles from **$$**.
WHERE TO EAT
Cosmopolitan Restaurant Western-saloon exterior; European-style cuisine from Hungarian chef Imi Kun. 1915 Wells Fargo Rd., Leeds, Utah; 435/879-6862; dinner for two †††.
Twentyfive Main Café with daily selection of house-baked cupcakes. 25 N. Main St., St. George, Utah; 435/628-7110; lunch for two †.
WHAT TO SEE & DO
Snow Canyon State Park Less crowded alternative to Zion. 1002 Snow Canyon Dr., Ivins, Utah; 435/628-2255.
Valley of Fire State Park Nevada's first state park, with some 35,000-odd acres of petroglyphs and dramatic rock formations. Overton, NV; 702/397-2088; parks.nv.gov.
Walking tour of St. George Ten-block self-guided tour featuring mid-1800's Mormon sites. Maps available at 1835 S. Convention Center Dr., St. George, Utah; 435/634-5747; utahsdixie.com.
Zion National Park Wade along the Virgin River in the famous hike known as the Narrows. Or for a quick overview, drive the Zion–Mt. Carmel highway from the western entrance. Springdale, Utah; 435/772-3256; nps.gov/zion.

IDAHO

WHERE TO STAY
Idaho Rocky Mountain Ranch Historic lodge and log cabins in the Sawtooth Range, with a natural hot spring and riding corral. Hwy. 75, Stanley; 208/774-3544; idahorocky.com; doubles from **$$**, including breakfast, packed lunch, and packed dinner.
South Fork Lodge Angler's idea of heaven, next to legendary fly-fishing on the South Fork of the Snake River. 40 Conant Valley Loop, Swan Valley; 877/347-4735 or 208/483-2112; southforklodge.com; doubles from **$$$**, including meals.
Wapiti Meadow Ranch Family-run guest ranch with horseback riding, fly-fishing, mountain biking, and hiking. 1667 Johnson Creek Rd., Cascade; 208/633-3217; wapitimeadowranch.com; doubles from **$$**, including all meals; three-night minimum.

SEATTLE

WHERE TO STAY
Inn at the Market Brick building in Pike Place Market, with rooms overlooking the city and Puget Sound. 86 Pine St.; 800/446-4484 or 206/443-3600; doubles from **$$**.
Hotel Monaco Pet-friendly boutique property whose design runs the gamut from cheery Mediterranean to boldly theatrical. 1101 Fourth Ave.; 800/945-2240 or 206/621-1770; monacoseattle.com; doubles from **$$$**.
WHERE TO SHOP
Glassybaby Airy boutique and glass blowing studio where customers can watch the line's colorful votives being made. 3406 E. Union St.; 206/568-7368.

DINING under $25→† $25-$74→†† $75–$149→††† $150–$299→†††† $300 + up→†††††

Hitchcock Handcrafted jewelry, vintage furnishings, accessories, and art in a space that changes its look seasonally. 1406 34th Ave.; 206/838-7173.

Pulp Lab Rotating collection of limited-edition items—from women's clothing to art—in a gallery-like setting. 5402 22nd Ave. N.W.; 206/706-7857.

Souvenir Found objects, collages, and clever tableaux tucked into display cabinets that serve as miniature installations. 5325 Ballard Ave. N.W.; 206/297-7116.

Velouria Girlish clothing, bags, and stationery, mostly by emerging Northwest designers. 2205 N.W. Market St.; 206/788-0330.

NAPA VALLEY, CA

WHERE TO STAY

Auberge du Soleil Elegant wine country escape with cottages tucked into a 33-acre olive grove. 180 Rutherford Hill Rd., Rutherford; 800/348-5406 or 707/963-1211; aubergedusoleil.com; doubles from **$$$$**.

Bardessono Eco-minded luxury at Napa's newest hotel; each room is like a private spa suite. 877/932-5333 or 707/204-6000; bardessono.com; doubles from **$$$**.

Poetry Inn Five-room vineyard retreat, with expansive bathrooms and jaw-dropping views. 6380 Silverado Trail, Napa; 707/944-0646; doubles from **$$$**, including breakfast.

WHERE TO EAT

Angèle Cozy converted boathouse serving bistro classics like pâté and cassoulet. 540 Main St., Napa; 707/252-8115; dinner for two ▮▮▮.

Bottega Napa Valley Food Network chef Michael Chiarello's latest restaurant, with a seasonal Italian menu. 6525 Washington St., Yountville; 707/945-1050; dinner for two ▮▮▮.

WHAT TO SEE & DO

Cade Winery Up Howell Mountain, an environmentally friendly new winery and tasting room. 360 Howell Mountain Rd., Angwin; 707/965-2746.

Round Pond Estate Olive oil, vinegars, and wines, with good guided tours. 886 Rutherford Rd., Rutherford; 888/302-2575.

LOS ANGELES

WHERE TO STAY

The Standard, Downtown L.A. The district's coolest hotel, in the Modernist Superior Oil headquarters. 550 S. Flower St.; 213/892-8080; standardhotels.com; doubles from **$$**.

Mondrian Designer Philippe Starck's signature look was recently updated by Benjamin Noriega-Ortiz. 8440 Sunset Blvd.; 323/650-8999; morganshotelgroup.com; doubles from **$$$**.

WHERE TO EAT

Clifton's Brookdale Cafeteria Depression-era landmark serving hearty, inexpensive fare in a kitschy woodland-inspired setting. 648 S. Broadway; 213/627-1673; dinner for two ▮.

WHAT TO SEE & DO

Bob Baker Marionette Theater Puppet extravaganza that's part Muppets, part Bolshoi Ballet. 1345 W. First St.; 213/250-9995; bobbakermarionettes.com.

Mayan Theater Historic movie house that hosts the cult favorite *Lucha Vavoom*. 1038 S. Hill St.; 213/746-4674; clubmayan.com.

Orpheum Theatre Former vaudeville venue; now the site of film festivals, awards shows, and rock concerts. 842 S. Broadway; 877/677-4386; laorpheum.com.

WHERE TO SHOP

Amoeba Music More than 250,000 titles on CD and vinyl. 6400 W. Sunset Blvd.; 323/245-6400.

dosa818 Loft atelier and boutique for designer Christina Kim's line, crafted from organic fabrics, environmentally friendly dyes, and recycled materials. 818 S. Broadway, 12th floor; 213/489-2801.

Echo Park Time Travel Mart Art installation that mimics a 1970's 7-Eleven, with "dinosaur eggs" and "robot milk" for sale. 1714 W. Sunset Blvd.; 213/413-3388.

NIGHTLIFE

The Edison Downtown club in a former abandoned power plant. 108 W. Second St.; 213/613-0000.

WAIKIKI, HI

WHERE TO STAY

Embassy Suites Waikiki Beach Walk On the southern end of the development, a 369-room all-suite property. 201 Beachwalk St.; 800/362-2779 or 808/921-2345; embassysuiteswaikiki.com; doubles from **$$**.

Halekulani Fabled hotel with gardens and a beachfront bar and restaurant. 2199 Kalia Rd.; 800/367-2343 or 808/923-2311; halekulani.com; doubles from **$$$**.

Kahala Hotel & Resort Classic Honolulu property that just underwent a soft redo—new beds, linens, and more. 5000 Kahala Ave.; 800/367-2525 or 808/739-8888; kahalaresort.com; doubles from **$$$**.

ALASKA

WHERE TO STAY

Alyeska Resort One of Alaska's poshest hotels, 40 miles southeast of Anchorage. 1000 Arlberg Ave., Girdwood; 800/880-3880 or 907/754-1111; alyeskaresort.com; doubles from **$$$**.

Camp Denali Deep inside the park; known for its summer lecture series. Denali National Park; 907/683-2290; campdenali.com; doubles from **$$$$$** for a three-night stay, including meals, transport to and from the park entrance, guided hiking trips, and natural history programs.

Redoubt Bay Lodge Small but pleasant lake-view cabins accessible only by seaplane. 907/274-2710; withinthewild.com; doubles from **$$$$$**, including meals, round-trip floatplane ride from Anchorage, and guided tours.

WHERE TO EAT

Seven Glaciers Fancy fare; killer views. At the top of Alyeska's aerial tramway; 907/754-2237; dinner for two ▮▮▮.

TRANSPORT

Alaska Railroad Book a glass-walled observation car from Anchorage to Denali National

Park. 800/544-0552; alaskarailroad.com.
Rust's Flying Service Seaplane tours and flights to Redoubt Bay Lodge and other camps. 800/544-2299 or 907/243-1595; flyrusts.com.

MONTREAL

WHERE TO STAY
Auberge Bonaparte Nineteenth-century hotel in a former judge's residence, overlooking the basilica of Notre-Dame. 447 Rue St.-François-Xavier; 514/844-1448; bonaparte.com; doubles from **$**.
WHERE TO EAT
Chez Gautier Latin Quarter brasserie with a sister patisserie next door. 3487 Ave. du Parc; 514/845-2992; dinner for two ❚❚.
L'Express Buzzing bistro serving straightforward, satisfying classics. 3927 Rue St.-Denis; 514/845-5333; dinner for two ❚❚.
Marché de la Villette Simple and traditional, with a good charcuterie selection. 324 Rue St-Paul Ouest; 514/807-8084; lunch for two ❚❚.
Olive et Gourmando Addictive baked goods, along with lunch items like soup and salads. 351 Rue St-Paul Ouest; 514/350-1083; lunch for two ❚.
WHAT TO SEE & DO
Fête des Neiges Annual outdoor celebrations of snow and ice in Parc Jean-Drapeau; held over three weekends in late January and early February. 514/872-6120; fetedes neiges.com.
Marché Bonsecours Neoclassical shopping emporium next to Notre

Dame. 350 rue St-Paul Est, Vieux Montréal; 514/872-7730.

NIAGARA FALLS

WHERE TO STAY
Harbour House Hotel Quiet luxury 20 minutes from the falls. 85 Melville St., Niagara-on-the-Lake; 866/277-6677 or 905/468-4683; harbourhousehotel.ca; doubles from **$$**.
Sheraton on the Falls High-rise hotel with jaw-dropping views. 5875 Falls Ave., Niagara Falls; 800/325-3535 or 905/374-4445; sheratononthefalls.com; doubles from **$**.
WHAT TO SEE & DO
Fort George National Historic Site British Army post during the War of 1812. Byron St., Niagara-on-the-Lake; 905/468-4257; pc.gc.ca.
Hillebrand Winery Creator of the region's first ice wine; call ahead for tours and wine seminars. 1249 Niagara Stone Rd., Niagara-on-the-Lake; 905/468-3201 or 800/582-8412; hillebrand.com.
Niagara Parks Botanical Gardens Arboretum, butterfly conservatory, and 100 acres of gardens ranging from Victorian roses to English herbs. 2565 North Niagara Pkwy., Niagara Falls; 905/356-8554; niagaraparks.com.
Skylon Tower View the falls from 775 feet up. 5200 Robinson St., Niagara Falls; 905/356-2651; skylon.com.
Whirlpool Jet Boat Tours Thrilling hour-long rides depart from Niagara-on-the-Lake. 888/438-4444; whirlpooljet.com; reservations required.

THE CARIBBEAN

SAN JUAN

WHERE TO STAY
Condado Plaza Hotel & Casino Affordable hotel with recently revamped rooms. 999 Ashford Ave.; 866/317-8934 or 787/721-1000; condadoplaza.com; doubles from **$$**.
La Concha Built in 1958 and fresh from a $220 million restoration, with many original design details intact. 1077 Ashford Ave. 877/524-7778 or 787/721-8500; laconcharesort.com; doubles from **$$**.
WHERE TO EAT
Budatai *Iron Chef* veteran Roberto Treviño's Asian-Latin hot spot. 1056 Ashford Ave.; 787/725-6919; dinner for two ❚❚❚.
Perla Seafood served under a colossal concrete conch shell (which gives La Concha hotel its name). 1077 Ashford Ave.; 787/721-7500; dinner for two ❚❚❚.
Strip House Upscale steak house with a sexy, red-walled dining room. At the Condado Plaza Hotel & Casino. 999 Ashford Ave.; 787/722-0150; dinner for two ❚❚❚.
Ummo Argentinean Grill Traditional, meat-heavy dishes off the *parrilla*. 1351 Ashford Ave.; 787/722-1700; dinner for two ❚❚.
WHERE TO SHOP
Lisa Cappalli Sophisticated and feminine; lots of lace. 151 Ave. de Diego; 787/724-6575.
Nono Maldonado Glamorous clothing for men and women, from the island's most famous

designer. 1112 Ashford Ave.; 787/721-0456.

ANGUILLA

WHERE TO STAY
Cap Juluca Eighteen beach villas with a Moorish vibe. Maundays Bay; 888/858-5822 or 264/497-6666; capjuluca.com; doubles from **$$$$**.
CuisinArt Resort Greek Isles–inspired architecture, a top-notch spa, and its own hydroponic farm. Rendezvous Bay; 800/943-3210 or 264/498-2000; cuisinartresort.com; doubles from **$$$$**.
Malliouhana Hotel & Spa Mediterranean-style compound; a top island destination since 1984. Meads Bay; 800/835-0796 or 264/497-6111; malliouhana.com; doubles from **$$$$**.
Viceroy Anguilla New in 2009, a glass-walled hotel from L.A. designer Kelly Wearstler. 305/722-7407; viceroyanguilla.com; doubles from **$$$$**.

ST. LUCIA

WHERE TO STAY
Discovery at Marigot Bay Contemporary interiors on a secluded cove and marina. Marigot; 758/458-5300; discoverystlucia.com; doubles from **$$$**.
Fond Doux Holiday Plantation *Agriturismo*-style resort on a 135-acre cocoa plantation. Open to the public for tours and Creole meals. Soufriere; 758/459-7545; fonddouxestate.com; doubles from **$$**.
Jade Mountain Impeccable food, cutting-edge design, and open-air suites facing

🍽 **DINING**   under $25 →❚ $25–$74 →❚❚ $75–$149 →❚❚❚ $150–$299 →❚❚❚❚ $300 + up →❚❚❚❚❚

the sea at what's easily St. Lucia's most expensive resort. Soufriere; 800/223-1108 or 758/459-4000; jademountainstlucia.com; doubles from $$$$$.

WHERE TO EAT

The Club at Jade Mountain Worth the splurge for the Soufriere paella and the salad of organic micro-greens. Non-resort guests must make a reservation. Soufriere; 758/459-4000; jademountainstlucia.com; dinner for two ¶¶¶¶.

The Coal Pot Beloved land-mark at marina's edge in St. Lucia's bustling capital. Vigie Marina, Castries; 758/452-5566; dinner for two ¶¶¶.

Friday Night Fish Fry Weekly street carnival and barbecue blowout where revelers drink rum punch and devour plates of spiced fish and octopus stew. Anse la Raye; dinner for two ¶.

Rowley's Caribbean Café Harborfront haunt for terrific gelato (also try the passion fruit sorbet). The Marina at Marigot Bay Village; 758/458-3691; gelato for two ¶.

Plas Kassav Down-home bakery on the highway between Soufriere and Anse la Raye; famous for dense, flavorful discs of cassava bread sprinkled with raisins or (for the bold) saltfish. Anse la Verdure; cassava breads ¶ each.

BARBADOS

WHERE TO STAY

Coral Reef Club Classic with a new two-story spa. St. James Beach; 800/223-1108 or 246/422-2372; coralreefbarbados.com; doubles from $$$$$.

The Crane One of the first resorts in the Caribbean; undergoing a multimillion-dollar expansion. St. Philip; 246/423-6220; thecrane.com; doubles from $$$.

Little Good Harbour Oceanfront cottages on the west coast. St. Peter; 246/439-3000; littlegood harbourbarbados.com; doubles from $$$.

Sandy Lane Longtime Caribbean retreat of the silk-cravat set, on a 1,000-acre stretch of white sand. Sandy Lane, St. James; 246/444-2000; sandylane.com; doubles from $$$$$.

Sea-U Guest House On the surfing coast. Tent Bay, Bathsheba, St. Joseph; 246/433-9450; seaubarbados.com; doubles from $.

WHERE TO EAT

Scarlet Late-night bistro with Anglophile leanings in menu and decor. Paynes Bay, St. James; 246/432-3663; dinner for two ¶¶¶.

WHAT TO SEE & DO

Open Houses Tours of historic homes every Wednesday from January through mid-April, hosted by the Barbados National Trust. 246/426-2421; barbados.org.

BEQUIA

WHERE TO STAY

Bequia Beach Hotel Colonial rooms with tropical accents; 29 more rooms slated to open in late 2009. Friendship; 784/458-1600; bequiabeach.com; doubles from $$.

Firefly Bequia Four luxurious rooms; sister property to the resort on neighboring Mustique. Spring; 784/458-3414; fireflybequia.com; doubles from $$$, all-inclusive.

WHERE TO EAT

Fernando's Hideaway The freshest fish, caught each morning by chef-owner Fernando Morgan. Lower Bay; 784/458-3758; dinner for two ¶¶.

WHERE TO SHOP

Sargeant Bros. Model Boats Miniature wooden whaling vessels crafted by a band of relatives in this house turned shop off Admiralty Bay. Port Elizabeth; 781/458-3344.

MUSTIQUE

WHERE TO STAY

Cotton House Rooms with breezy verandas, private decks, and beds draped in netting; two restaurants and a spa, plus snorkeling right offshore. 888/452-8380 or 784/456-4777; cottonhouse.net; doubles from $$$$$.

Firefly Mustique Airy five-room guesthouse with island touches, like a sea pebble shower and a patio hammock. 784/488-8414; fireflymustique.com; doubles from $$$$.

The Mustique Company For villa rentals. 800/747-9214; mustique-island.com.

NIGHTLIFE

Basil's Bar The Caribbean's most iconic hangout. 784/488-8350.

San Juan

Anguilla

St. Lucia

Mustique

Barbados

Bequia

Grenada

GRENADA

WHERE TO STAY

Laluna Resort Sixteen cottages, each with its own plunge pool and wide veranda. Morne Rouge, St. George's; 866/452-5862 or 473/439-0001; laluna.com; cottages from $$$$.

Mount Cinnamon Beach Resort One-bedroom suites and villas on Grand Anse Beach. Morne Rouge, St. George's; 866/720-2616 or 473/439-9900; mount cinnamongrenada.com; doubles from $$$.

WHERE TO EAT

Aquarium On Point Salines Beach, a thatched-roof restaurant and popular beach bar that hosts a festive Sunday barbecue. Magazine Beach; 473/444-1410; dinner for two ¶¶.

Gouyave Fish Fridays Streets lined with vendors hawking irresistible seafood specialties. St. Francis and St. Dominic streets, Gouyave; dinner for two ¶.

WHERE TO SHOP

Tikal Locally made baskets, clothing, and jewelry. Young St., St. George's; 473/440-2310.

THE CARIBBEAN

LODGING under $150 →$ $150—$299 → $$ $300—$699 → $$$ $700—$999 → $$$$ $1,000 + up →$$$$$

Baja California

Belize

Mazatlán

Valle de Bravo

Cuernavaca

Nicaragua

Guatemala

Nicoya Peninsula

Tranco

Atacama Desert

Cachi

MEXICO +
CENTRAL
+ SOUTH
AMERICA

MEXICO + CENTRAL + SOUTH AMERICA

BAJA CALIFORNIA, MEXICO

WHERE TO STAY
Moorings Charter company for yachts and catamarans, equipped with sleeping cabins and provisions. 888/952-8420; moorings.com; four-person catamarans from **$$$** per day.

WHAT TO SEE & DO
Fun Baja Snorkeling and diving equipment for rent. Marina Costa Baja, Km. 6.5, Carr. a Pichilingue, La Paz; 52-612/106-7148; funbaja.com; equipment from **$** per person).

MAZATLÁN, MEXICO

WHERE TO STAY
Casa Lucila Old Town's first boutique hotel, built on the ruins of an 18th-century mansion. 16 Calle Olas Altas; 52-669/982-1100; casalucila.com; doubles from **$**.
Melville Suites Twenty airy suites in vibrant colors. 99 Avda. Constitución; 52-669/982-8474; themelville.com; doubles from **$**.

WHERE TO EAT
Pedro y Lola Regional dishes such as *molcajete* (chunks of *arrachera* beef with grilled nopales) served in a 130-year-old building. Avdas. Constitución and Carnaval; 52-669/982-2589; dinner for two 🍴🍴.

WHAT TO SEE & DO
Teatro Ángela Peralta Hosts dance performances, concerts, and avant-garde plays. 1024 Calle Carnaval; 52-669/982-4446.

WHERE TO SHOP
Casa Etnika Artist-owned gallery in Old Town. 50 Calle Sixto Osuna; 52-669/136-0139.

VALLE DE BRAVO, MEXICO

WHERE TO STAY & EAT
Rodavento Boutique Hotel Glass-walled property edging the lake. Km 3.5, Carr. Los Saucos-Valle de Bravo; 52-726/251-4182; rodavento.com; doubles from **$$**.
Dipao Pizza y Vino Reliable Italian. 100 Joaquín Arcadio Pagaza; 52-726/262-2965; lunch for two 🍴.

WHAT TO SEE & DO
FlyMexico For paragliding lessons. 800/861-7198; flymexico.com.
Temple of Santa María Ahuacatlán Chapel built in the 1860's. Colonia Santa María.
Valle la Revista Tours of Lake Avándaro. Embarcadero Municipal S/N, in front of Capitania de Puerto; 52-726/262-2400; vallelarevista.com.
Yate Fiesta Valle Party boat. 5 Misión; 52-726/262-0558.

CUERNAVACA, MEXICO

WHERE TO STAY
Hotel Villa Béjar Rooms overlooking gardens, and a spa. 2350 Avda. Domingo Díez, Colonia Chamilpa; 52-777/101-0000; villabejar.com.mx; doubles from **$**.

Las Mañanitas Grand hotel with a can't-miss restaurant (try the *cochinita pibil*). 107 Calle Ricardo Linares; 52-777/362-0000; las mananitas.com.mx; doubles from **$$**.

WHERE TO EAT
Los Arcos Café on the main square that's open until midnight. 4 Jardín de los Héroes; 52-777/312-1510; lunch for two 🍴.

WHAT TO DO
Cuauhnáhuac Intensive Spanish Language School One-week and longer immersion programs for all levels. 123 Avda. Morelos Sur, Colonia Chipitlán; 52-777/312-3673; cuauhna huac.edu.mx.

BELIZE

WHERE TO STAY
Belize Zoo Dorm-style rooms or cabins on stilts for

family overnights. Mile 29, Western Hwy., Belize City; 011-501/220-8004; belize zoo.org; doubles from $.

Caves Branch Jungle Lodge Adventure-minded rain forest retreat. Mile 41.5, Hummingbird Hwy., Belmopan, Cayo District; 011-501/822-2800; caves branch.com; doubles from $, three-night minimum.

De Real Macaw Guest House Simple, centrally located cabanas with bunk beds and hammocks, or rooms in an air-conditioned guesthouse. Avda. Hicaco, Caye Caulker; 011-501/226-0459; derealmacaw.biz; cabanas from $.

NIGHTLIFE

I&I Reggae Bar Unwind in a hammock on the roof. Off Front St., Caye Caulker; 011-501/625-0344.

GUATEMALA

WHERE TO STAY

Hotel Casa Santo Domingo Seventeenth-century former convent and Antigua's finest accommodations. 28 Calle 3ª Oriente, Antigua; 502/7820-1220; casasanto domingo.com.gt; doubles from $.

Hotel Casa Vecchia Meticulously restored four-room gem. 16 Avda. 5ª Sur, Antigua; 502/7832-3055; hotelcasavecchia.com; doubles from $$.

WHERE TO EAT

La Cuevita de los Urquizu Serving chapina cuisine near the Convento de Santa Clara. 9D Calle 2ª Oriente, Antigua; dinner for two ⏐.

WHAT TO SEE & DO

Chichicastenango Highland town famous for its Mayan market of traditional handicrafts and local goods.

Convent of Santa Clara Ruins of a church and cloister, including a two-tiered arcade and fountain. Avda. 2ª at Calle 6ª Oriente, Antigua.

Iglesia El Calvario Colonial church with frescoes. End of Alameda El Calvario, Antigua.

Iglesia Santo Tomás Four-hundred-year-old church next to the plaza where the market is held. Plaza del Municipio, Chichicastenango.

Palacio de los Capitanes Generales Former seat of Spanish colonial power in Latin America. Calle 5ª Poniente, between Avda. 4ª and Avda. 5ª, Antigua.

Palacio Nacional Ornate state building completed in 1943; now houses a collection of Guatemalan art. Calle 6ª and Avda. 7ª, Plaza Mayor, Guatemala City.

NICARAGUA

WHERE TO STAY

Casa Canada Low-key beach resort with all the tropical trappings—terra-cotta tile rooms, a bar on the beach, hammocks, and an infinity pool. South End, Big Corn Island; 011-514/448-8339; casa-canada.com; doubles from $.

Morgan's Rock Hacienda & Ecolodge Nicaragua's chicest and most eco-conscious spot to sleep. San Juan del Sur; 505/2254-7989; morgansrock.com; doubles from $$$, all-inclusive.

WHERE TO EAT

Anastasia's on the Sea Quintessentially Caribbean restaurant on the end of a pier, serving lobster, fried shrimp, and Toña beer.

Costa Norte, Big Corn Island; 011-505/937-0016; dinner for two ⏐.

NICOYA PENINSULA, COSTA RICA

WHERE TO STAY

El Sueño Tropical Low-key camp a mile and a half from the beach; rooms are set on a hill, surrounded by flower gardens. Playa Carillo; 877/456-4338 or 506/2656-0151; elsuenotropical.com; doubles from $.

Hotel Playa Negra Simple bungalows and a surf school. Two and a half miles northwest of Paraíso, on a dirt road (watch for signs); 506/2652-9134; playanegra.com; bungalows for four $.

WHERE TO EAT

Café Playa Negra Tico and Peruvian fare. Main Street, Playa Negra; 506/2652-9351; dinner for two ⏐.

Lola's Funky lunch spot on Playa Avellana. 506/2658-8097; lunch for two ⏐.

ATACAMA DESERT, CHILE

WHERE TO STAY

Tierra Atacama Hotel & Spa High-design adventure resort with a staff of expert guides. 800/829-5325 or 56-2/263-0606; tierraatacama.com; doubles from $$$, including breakfast and use of the spa.

CACHI, ARGENTINA

WHERE TO STAY

Estancia Colomé Luxurious suites and a picturesque

pool on a remote 96,000-acre compound. Km 20, Ruta Provincial 53, Molinos; 54-3868/494-044; estanciacolome.com; doubles from $$.

La Merced del Alto Panoramic views from a Spanish colonial-style hacienda. Fuerte Alto, Cachi; 54-3868/490-030; lamerceddelalto.com; doubles from $.

WHERE TO EAT

Luna Cautiva Authentic *salteña* cuisine in a 1796 building. Calle Bojas Díaz, Cachi; 54-3868/491-029; dinner for two ⏐⏐.

Oliver Wine Bar Pizza and tapas downstairs; Colomé vintages upstairs in the cozy bar. 160 Avda. Ruíz de los Llanos; 54-3868/491-903; dinner for two ⏐.

WHAT TO SEE & DO

Mercado Artesanal Local crafters sell their wares at this municipal market. Avda. General Güemes; 54-3868/491-221.

TRANCOSO, BRAZIL

WHERE TO STAY

Pousada Etnia Eight-villa resort with rooms done up in various styles—from Moroccan and Goan to Japanese and African tribal. 25 Avda. Principal; 55-73/3668-1137; etnia brasil.com.br; villas from $$, including breakfast.

Uxua Casa Boutique hotel opened by Diesel creative director Wilbert Das, with six villas around a garden and another three villas facing the town square. On the Quadrado; 55-73/3668-2166; uxua.com.br; doubles from $$$, including breakfast.

EUROPE

LONDON

WHERE TO STAY
Main House Notting Hill Victorian with a posh home-away-from-home feel. 6 Colville Rd.; 44-20/7221-9691; themainhouse.co.uk; doubles from **$**.

Waldorf Hilton In the heart of the West End; take tea 1920's-style in the Homage Patisserie. Aldwych; 44-20/7759-4083; hilton.co.uk; doubles from **$$**.

WHERE TO EAT
Geales Revived Notting Hill classic with the freshest fish-and-chips. 2 Farmer St.; 44-20/7727-7528; dinner for two ||| .

Treacle Takeaway teas and nostalgic baked goods. 110–112 Columbia Rd.; 44-20/7729-0538; snacks for two | .

WHERE TO SHOP
Hope and Greenwood Old-fashioned sweetshop. 1 Russell St.; 44-20/7240-3314.

NIGHTLIFE
Bourne & Hollingsworth Louche basement bar in Fitzrovia. 28 Rathbone Place; 44-20/7636-8228.

Rivoli Ballroom Classic dance floor with swing nights. 346–350 Brockley Rd.; 44-20/8692-5130.

THE COTSWOLDS, ENGLAND

WHERE TO STAY
Barnsley House Boutique property with a B&B Italia–furnished spa and gardens by landscape designer Rosemary Verey. Hwy. B4425, near Bibury,

Gloucestershire; 44-1285/740-000; www.barnsley house.com; doubles from **$$$**.

Cotswolds88 Hotel Loungy electronic background music, on-trend upholsteries, and eclectic antiques in the common areas. Kemps Lane, Painswick, Gloucestershire; 44-1452/813-688; cotswolds88hotel.com; doubles from **$$**.

Cowley Manor Circa-16th-century country house with an irreverent vibe, on 55 acres with two pools and an award-winning spa. Cowley, Gloucestershire; 44-1224/870-900; cowleymanor. com; doubles from **$$$**.

WHERE TO EAT
The Swan at Southrop Husband-and-wife–run gastropub on a village green. Southrop, Gloucestershire; 44-1367/850-205; dinner for two ||| .

Trouble House Headed by a Marco Pierre White–trained chef from London, with a focus on local ingredients. Cirencester Rd., near Tetbury, Gloucestershire; 44-1666/502-206; dinner for two ||| .

WHAT TO SEE & DO
Merriscourt Arts Centre Estate and farmland with a host of new enterprises, from an art gallery to a recording studio. Merriscourt,

Chipping Norton, Oxfordshire; 44-7970/547-765; merriscourt.com.

WHERE TO SHOP
Highgrove Shop Organic foods and lifestyle goods; profits benefit Prince Charles's foundation. 10 Long St., Tetbury, Gloucestershire; 44-1666/505-666.

ENGLISH COUNTRYSIDE

WHERE TO STAY
Feather Down Farms Holiday stays in rural tents on homesteads around England and Scotland.

DINING under $25 →| $25–$74 →|| $75–$149 →||| $150–$299 →|||| $300 + up →|||||

44-1420/80804; feather down.co.uk; tents from **$$**.

ISLE OF SKYE, SCOTLAND

WHERE TO STAY

The House Over-By Six-room inn that exudes understated romance. Colbost, Dunvegan; 44-1470/511-258; three chimneys.co.uk; doubles from **$$**.

Stein Inn Sample the bar's vast inventory of single malts, then settle into one of five rooms. MacLeod's Terrace, Waternish; 44-1470/592-362; steininn.co.uk; doubles from **$**.

Kinloch Lodge Cookbook author Lady Claire MacDonald's haven. Off A851, Sleat Peninsula; 44-1471/833-333; kinloch-lodge.co.uk; doubles from **$$**, including breakfast and dinner.

WHERE TO EAT

Three Chimneys Restaurant Destination dining, next to the House Over-By. Colbost, Dunvegan; 44-1470/511-258; threechimneys.co.uk; dinner for two **�‖�‖❙**.

WHAT TO SEE & DO

Talisker Distillery The Isle of Skye's sole distillery, producing a peaty scotch not for the faint of heart. Carbost; 44-1478/614-308.

IRELAND

WHERE TO STAY

Glasshouse Hotel Fresh and modern, on the River Garavogue. Swan Point, Sligo; 353-71/919-4300; theglasshouse.ie; doubles from **$**, including breakfast.

Knockranny House Hotel & Spa Book one of the oldest rooms, and consider dining in. Castlebar Rd., Westport, Co. Mayo; 353-98/28600; khh.ie; doubles from **$**.

NIGHTLIFE

Ceolaras Coleman Music Centre Brick structure with classrooms, a small shop, and a concert hall. Gurteen, Co. Sligo; 353-71/918-2599; colemanirishmusic.com.

Matt Molloy's Traditional Irish music nightly in a festive atmosphere. Bridge St., Westport, Co. Mayo; 353-098/26655.

McGarrigles Pub Performances on Wednesdays and Thursdays. O'Connell St., Sligo; 353-71/917-1193.

Shoot the Crows Music on Tuesdays and Wednesdays. Market Cross, Sligo; no phone.

WHAT TO SEE & DO

Corcomroe Abbey Brooding, atmospheric ruins of a 12th-century abbey. Ballyvaughan.

PARIS

WHERE TO STAY

Apostrophe Hotel New boutique hotel near the heart of Montparnasse; each room is designed around a poem. 3 Rue de Chevreuse, Sixth Arr.; 33-1/56-54-31-31; apostrophe-hotel.com; doubles from **$$$**.

Hotel Thérèse Elegantly furnished rooms in an 18th-century townhouse. 5–7 Rue Therese, First Arr.; 33-1/42-96-10-01; hoteltherese.com; doubles from **$$**.

WHERE TO EAT

Afaria Basque bistro with a playful menu. 15 Rue Desnouettes, 15th Arr.; 33-1/48-56-15-36; dinner for two **❙❙❙**.

Itinéraires Market-driven fare. 5 Rue de Pontoise, Fifth Arr.; 33-1/46-33-60-11; dinner for two **❙❙❙**.

L'Agassin Innovative spin on traditional French cooking. 8 Rue Malar, Seventh Arr.; 33-1/47-05-18-18; dinner for two **❙❙**.

THE PYRENEES, FRANCE

WHERE TO STAY

Château de Beauregard Revamped and romantic 19th-century château with exquisite Gascon cuisine. Ave. de la Résistance, St.-Girons; 33-5/61-66-66-64; chateaubeauregard.net; doubles from **$**.

Farm Stays Lodging in the homes of property owners in Ariège who take in guests during the transhumance. Contact the Office de Tourisme de St.-Girons et du Couserans. 33-5/61-96-26-60; transh couserans.com.

WHAT TO SEE & DO

Ariège Transhumance The most visitor-friendly of the animal migrations open to the public. May 30–June 14; 33-5/61-96-26-60; transh couserans.com.

AIX-EN-PROVENCE, FRANCE

WHERE TO STAY

28 à Aix Intimate hotel in the city center. 28 Rue du 4 Septembre, Aix; 33-4/42-54-82-01; 28aaix.com; doubles from **$$$**.

La Pauline B&B on 20 acres of gardens. Les Pinchinats, 280 Chemin de la Fontaine des Tuiles, Aix; 33-4/42-17-02-60; lapauline.fr; doubles from **$$**.

Here and Abroad Villa rentals in the Aix area and other Provençal towns; excellent, personalized service. 610/228-4984; hereandabroad.com.

WHERE TO EAT

L'Hostellerie de l'Abbaye de la Celle Alain Ducasse–run restaurant and inn in a 12th-century former Benedictine abbey, with umbrella-shaded tables in a garden. 10 Place du General de Gaulle, La Celle; 33-4/98-05-14-14; dinner for two **❙❙❙**.

WHAT TO SEE & DO

Aix Farmers' Market One-stop shopping for the loca-vore set. Place Richelme; 8 a.m. to 1 p.m. daily.

Cooking with Friends in France Culinary-immersion classes. Plascassier; cook ingwithfriends.com; six-day programs from **$$$$$**.

BASQUE COUNTRY, FRANCE

WHERE TO STAY & EAT

Hegia Only guests of the five-room bed-and-breakfast can dine at the Michelin-starred restaurant. Quartier Zelai, Hasparren; 33-5/59-29-67-86; hegia.com; doubles from **$$$**, including break-fast and dinner.

Hôtel Arraya Quaint and centrally located. Place du Village, Sare; 33-5/59-54-20-46; arraya.com; doubles from **$$**; dinner for two **❙❙**.

L'Auberge Basque Southern France's best new restaurant, plus a nine-room inn with bespoke interiors. D307 Vieille Route de St.-Jean-de-Luz, St.-Pée-sur-Nivelle; 33-5/59-51-70-00; aubergebasque.com; doubles from $; dinner for two ❚❚❚.

WHERE TO EAT
Etche-Ona Family-owned bistro across from the Basque pelota court. 15 Place Floque, St.-Jean-Pied-de-Port; 33-5/59-37-01-14; lunch for two ❚❚.

WHERE TO SHOP
Chocolatier Antton Artisanal chocolate shop showcasing regional specialties. Place du Marché, Espelette; 33-5/59-93-88-72.

MADRID

WHERE TO STAY
Hotel Ritz Lavish Belle Époque style, from the soaring ceilings to the antique furnishings. 5 Plaza de la Lealtad; 800/237-1236 or 34/91-701-6767; ritzmadrid.com; doubles from $$$.
Hotel Alicia Crisp and contemporary, with floor-to-ceiling windows and flat-screen TV's. 2 Calle Prado; 34/91-389-6095; room-matehotels.com; doubles from $.

WHERE TO EAT
Astrid & Gastón Madrid Posh Peruvian import where ceviche is the star. 13 Paseo de la Castellana; 34/91-702-6262; dinner for two ❚❚❚.
DiverXo Imaginative palate-teasers in an unlikely neighborhood. 5 Calle Francisco Medrano; 34/91-570-0766; dinner for two ❚❚❚❚.
Kabuki Wellington Starkly handsome temple to sushi, with sticker-shock prices. 6 Calle Velásquez; 34/91-577-7877; dinner for two ❚❚❚❚.

Sula Tapas bar, restaurant, and food shop that's a favorite of Madrid's celebrity set. 33 Calle Jorge Juan; 34/91-781-6197; dinner for two ❚❚❚❚.
Zaranda Michelin-starred nook from the city's most buzzed-about restaurant couple. 5 Paseo Eduardo Dato; 34/91-446-4548; dinner for two ❚❚❚❚.

RIOJA, SPAIN

WHERE TO STAY
Hotel Marqués de Riscal Frank Gehry's signature design includes an innovative restaurant and a spa. 1 Calle Torrea, Elciego; 800/325-3589 or 34/94-518-0880; luxurycollection.com; doubles from $$$.
Hotel Marqués de Vallejo Elegant 50-room property in the center of the old town. 8 Calle Marqués de Vallejo, Logroño; 34/94-124-8333; doubles from $$.

WHERE TO EAT & DRINK
Bar Sebas Storefront-size watering hole with a formidable list of wines. 3 Calle Albornoz, Logroño; 34/94-122-0196; tapas for two ❚.
Bar Soriano Order the shrimp and mushrooms cooked with garlic. 2 Travesía del Laurel, Logroño; 34/94-122-8807; tapas for two ❚.
Blanco y Negro Irresistible *matrimonio* sandwiches: roasted peppers and salted anchovy on a soft bun. 1 Travesía del Laurel, Logroño; 34/94-122-0079; tapas for two ❚.
Electra Rioja Gran Casino Sleek, postmodern boîte in a small casino. 10 Calle Sagasta, Logroño; 34/94-125-1420; tapas for two ❚.

DOURO VALLEY, PORTUGAL

WHERE TO STAY & WHAT TO DO
Quinta da Romaneira Luxe 19-room manor with a wine cellar converted to a pool and hammam. Cotas; 351-25/473-2432; www.maisondesreves.com; doubles from $$$$$, all-inclusive.
Quinta do Vallado Ocher-color manor on a centuries-old vineyard producing promising young table wines. Vilarinho des Freieres, Peso da Régua; 351-25/432-3147; quinta dovallado.com; doubles from $.

LAKE COMO, ITALY

WHERE TO STAY
Grand Hotel Villa Serbelloni Sumptuous 19th-century hotel and spa on a private shoreline. 1 Via Roma, Bellagio; 39-031/950-216; villaserbelloni.com; doubles from $$$.
Villa d'Este Unparalleled grandeur, with an exclusive guest list. 40 Via Regina, Cernobbio; 800/223-6800 or 39-010/031-3481; villadeste.it; doubles from $$$$.

WHAT TO SEE & DO
Villa Carlotta Statues, a stone tower, and an exotic rain forest. 2 Via Regina, Tremezzo; 39-03/444-0405; villacarlotta.it.
Villa del Balbianello Eclectic mix of French, English, and Italian influences. Via Comoedia, Lenno; 39-03/445-6110; fondo ambiente.it.
Villa Melzi Park-like grounds with towering

North American trees. 22021 Lungolario Manzoni, Bellagio; 39-02/8699-8647; giardinidivillamelzi.it.

VENICE

WHERE TO STAY
Ca' Sagredo Magnificently frescoed palazzo on the Grand Canal. Book Suite 316 for walls covered in mythological works dating back to the 1700's, by artists Abbondio Stazio and Carpoforo Mazzetti. Campo Santa Sofia, Cannaregio 4198–99; 800/525-4800 or 39-041/241-3111; casagredohotel.com; doubles from $$$.
IQs Accessible by gondola, a four-room boutique hotel done up in contemporary furnishings by Moroso and B&B Italia. Campiello Querini Stampalia, Castello 4425; 866/376-7831 or 39-041/241-0062; thecharminghouse.com; doubles from $$.
Oltre il Giardino Six-room villa within a garden in the historic center. Fondamenta Contarini, San Polo 2542; 39-041/275-0015; www.oltreilgiardino-venezia.com; doubles from $$.

WHERE TO EAT
Osteria Alle Testiere Retro bistro with some of Venice's most coveted tables. Calle del Mondo Novo, Castello 5801; 39-041/522-7220; dinner for two ❚❚❚.
Pronto Pesce Pronto Picnic provisions at a delicatessen specializing in seafood. Pescheria Rialto, San Polo 2202A; 39-041/822-0298; dinner for two ❚❚.

WHERE TO SHOP
Fortuny Factory and Showroom Textile heaven, founded by designer

DINING under $25 → ❚ $25–$74 → ❚❚ $75–$149 → ❚❚❚ $150–$299 → ❚❚❚❚ $300 + up → ❚❚❚❚❚

Mariano Fortuny; open by appointment. Giudecca 805; 39-041/528-7697.

Giovanna Zanella Vibrant colors and avant-garde custom styles from a master cobbler. Campo San Lio, Castello 5641; 39-041/523-5500.

Legatoria Polliero Workshop specializing in notebooks, wrapping paper, and picture frames. Campo dei Frari, San Polo 2995; 39-041/528-5130.

Madera Contemporary housewares ranging from teapots to wooden bowls. Campo San Barnaba, Dorsoduro 2762; 39-041/522-4181.

Tessitura Luigi Bevilacqua Textile workshop frequented by both Vatican priests and local fashion designers. Campiello della Comar, Santa Croce 1320; 39-041/721-566; by appointment.

NIGHTLIFE

Harry's Bar Watering hole with an A-list following and a legendary atmosphere, plus bragging rights for having invented the Bellini. Calle Vallaresso, San Marco 1323; 39-041/528-5777.

ROME

WHERE TO STAY

Casa di Santa Brigida Convent hotel run by nuns. 54 Via Mon Serrato; 39-06/6889-2596; brigidine.org; doubles from **$$$$**.

Hotel Santa Maria Cloister turned hotel in Trastevere; junior suites are ideal for families of four. 2 Vicolo del Piede; 39-06/589-4626; hotelsantamaria.info; doubles from **$**.

WHERE TO EAT

Da Baffetto Busy dinner-only pizzeria off the famous Campo de' Fiori. 114 Via del Governo Vecchio; 39-06/686-1617; dinner for two $.

Giolitti Famous gelato parlor near the Piazza Colonna. 40 Via Uffici del Vicaro; 39-06/699-1243.

WHAT TO SEE & DO

Great Synagogue On the banks of the Tiber, overlooking the Ghetto Vecchio, with the city's only squared dome; home to the Jewish Museum. Lungotevere Cenci; 39-06/6840-0651.

St. Peter's Basilica Awe-inspiring history and architecture; one of Italy's most venerated sights. Piazza San Pietro, Vatican City; 39-06/6988-1662; saintpetersbasilica.org.

CILENTO COAST, ITALY

WHERE TO STAY

Il Cannito Intimate bed-and-breakfast run by a local chef and her three children, with a private lido on the beach near the temples at Paestum. Via Cannito, Capaccio-Paestum; 39-0828/196-2277; ilcannito.com; doubles from **$$**.

Palazzo Belmonte Monumental stone palace and gardens overlooking the water. 25 Via Flavio Gioia, Santa Maria di Castellabate; 39-0974/960-211; palazzo belmonte.com; doubles from **$$**.

WHERE TO EAT

Ristorante Il Caicco Dine on a garden terrace high above the sea. 5 Via San Biagio, Castellabate; 39-0974/843-044; dinner for two $$$$.

U' Mazzeno Seafood specialties in a colorful osteria. Via Provinciale, Ogliastro Marina, Castellabate; 39-0974/963-522; dinner for two $$$.

WHERE TO SHOP

Tenuta Vannulo Organic buffalo milk products, including a *mozzarella di bufala* that's usually sold out before noon. Via G. Galilei, Capaccio-Paestum; 39-0828/724-765.

ENGADINE VALLEY, SWITZERLAND

WHERE TO STAY

Engadin St. Moritz Tourism Organization House rentals all over the valley. 41-81/830-0001; www.engadin.ch.

Hotel Castell Newly refurbished, hip yet family-friendly. Zuoz; 41-81/851-5253; hotelcastell.ch; doubles from **$**.

WHERE TO SHOP

COOP Good local supermarket for stocking up on vacation-house provisions. 1 Crappun, Samedan; 41-81/851-0050.

WHAT TO SEE & DO

Alp-Shaukäserei Morteratsch Watch sheep's-milk cheese made in the traditional manner. Sennereiggenossenschaft, Pontresina; 41-81/842-6273; alp-schaukaeserei.ch.

Willy Sport Bicyle rentals just off the bike path outside Zuoz. Chesa La Tuor; 41-81/854-1289; willy-sport.ch.

RHINE VALLEY, GERMANY

WHERE TO STAY

Hotel Eisenhut In four former mansions near the central market. Herrngasse 3-5/7, Rothenberg; 49-9861/7050; eisenhut.com; doubles from **$**.

Hotel Elephant Sixteenth-century structure with polished interiors and one of Germany's best restaurants. 19 Markt, Weimar; 800/325-3589 or 49-3643/8020; luxury collection.com; doubles from **$**.

Schönburg Castle Hotel Wood-paneled rooms in an ancient former fortress. Oberwesel; 49-6744/93930; hotel-schoenburg.com; doubles from **$$**, including breakfast.

WHERE TO EAT

Historische Weinwirtschaft Laid-back atmosphere and a locally made sauerbraten. 17 Liebfrauen Str., Oberwesel; 49-6744/8186; dinner for two $$.

Restaurant Mittermeier Underneath a more formal dining room, a basement eatery swarming with young locals. 9 Vorm Wurzburger Tor, Rothenburg; 49-9861/94540; dinner for two $$$.

WHAT TO SEE & DO

Heidelberg Castle Built in the 12th century, and torn apart by years of warfare. Heidelberg; 49-6221/538-414; visit-heidelberg.com.

Hornberg Castle High above a forest, the oldest castle in the Neckar Valley. Neckarzimmern; 49-6261/92460; burg-hotel-hornberg.de.

BERLIN

WHERE TO STAY

Art'Otel Modern and colorful, inspired by the works of Andy Warhol. 85 Lietzenburger Strasse; 49-30/887-7770; artotel.de; doubles from **$**.

LODGING

under $150 → **$** $150–$299 → **$$** $300–$699 → **$$$** $700–$999 → **$$$$** $1,000 + up → **$$$$$**

Hotel Adlon Kempinski Berlin Historic property just steps from the Brandenburg Gate. 77 Unter den Linden; 49-30/884-340; hotel-adlon.de; doubles from $$$.

WHERE TO EAT

Defne Restaurant Near the Turkish market; serving Mediterranean-style dishes like lamb skewers, aubergines with pine nuts and peppers, and a spicy octopus. 92C Planufer; 49-30/8179-7111; dinner for two ❙❙.

WHAT TO SEE & DO

Kaiser Wilhelm Memorial Church Evocatively rebuilt reminder of the devastation of war. Breitscheidplatz, Charlottenberg; 49-30/218-5023.

Memorial to the Murdered Jews of Europe Powerfully abstract and haunting, a vast expanse of concrete slabs in the city center. Edge of Grosser Tiergarten, between Wilhelmstrasse and Eberstrasse; stiftung-denkmal.de.

Reischstag Historic building topped with a transparent Norman Foster dome. Platz der Republik; 49-30/2270; bundestag.de.

Turkish Market Along the Landwehrkanal; every Tuesday and Friday from noon till 6:30 p.m. Maybachufer, on the border of Kreuzberg and Neukölln.

NIGHTLIFE

Ankerklause Popular (read: packed) watering hole on a boat overlooking the Landwehrkanal. Kottbusser Brücke, corner of Maybachufer, Neukölln; 49-30/693-5649.

Berghain Massive warehouse club at the center of Berlin's after-hours scene. Am Wriezener Bahnhof.

KMA 36 Two-level bar in a striking glass cube. 36 Karl-Marx-Allee.

THE NETHERLANDS

WHERE TO STAY

Hotel New York Former headquarters of the Holland-America line; lofty rooms filled with primary-color furniture. 1 Koninginnenhoofd, Rotterdam; 31-10/439-0500; hotelnewyork.nl; doubles from $.

Sofitel Amsterdam the Grand Centrally located 15th-century convent transformed into a high-service hotel. 197 Oudezijds Voorburgwal, Amsterdam; 31-20/555-3111; sofitel.com; doubles from $$$.

WHERE TO EAT

De Bakkerswinkel Rustic yet elegant bakery featuring pieces of furniture by design star Piet Hein Eek. 69 Warmoesstraat; 31-20/489-8000; lunch for two ❙.

WHERE TO SHOP

Frozen Fountain Furniture and textiles from some of Holland's biggest names. 645 Prinsengracht, Amsterdam; 31-20/622-9375.

Galerie Animaux Mix of emerging artists and designers. 15 Van Vollenhovenstraat, Rotterdam; 31-10/243-0043.

Studio Hergebruik Wacky collection of objects, clothing, and accessories. 53 Coolsingel, Rotterdam; 31-10/413-3660.

COPENHAGEN

WHERE TO STAY

Copenhagen Admiral Hotel Warehouse turned 366-room property. 24–28 Toldbodgade; 45/3374-1414; admiralhotel.dk; doubles from $$.

Hotel Fox Affordable rooms designed by international artists. 3 Jarmers Plads; 45/3313-3000; hotelfox.dk; doubles from $.

WHAT TO SEE & DO

Black Diamond Striking granite-clad extension to the Royal Library thrusts right out to the waterfront. 1 Søren Kierkegaards Plads; 45/3347-4747; kb.dk.

Fisketorvet Byens Shopping Center Modern shopping mall in a former fish market. 59 Kalvebod Brygge; 45/3336-6400; fisketorvet.dk.

Frøsiloen Gemini Residences Abandoned silos converted into cutting-edge apartments. Islands Brygge.

Operaen Imposing opera house at the center of the waterfront development. 10 Ekvipagemestervej; 45/3369-6969; kglteater.dk.

Royal Danish Playhouse Huge glass windows front the main harbor and Nyhavn Canal. 36 Sankt Annæ Plads; 45/3369-6969; kglteater.dk.

NORWAY

WHERE TO STAY

Det Hanseatiske Hotel Wood-beamed former trading house constructed after the great fire of 1702. 2A Finnegaarden, Bergen; 47-5/530-4800; dethanseatiskehotell.no; doubles from $$.

First Hotel Grims Grenka High-design newcomer with iPod docking stations, Bang & Olufsen televisions, and an organic restaurant. 5 Kongens Gate, Oslo; 47-2/310-7200; grimsgrenka.no; doubles from $$$.

WHERE TO EAT

Bagatelle Feast on attention-getting cuisine from chef Eyvind Hellstrøm at this Michelin-starred spot. 3 Bygdøy Alle, Oslo; 47-2/212-1440; dinner for two ❙❙❙.

Godt Brød Popular café and bakery serving excellent coffee, fresh pastries, and sandwiches made with organic ingredients. 2 Vestre Torggate, Bergen; 47-5/556-3310; lunch for two ❙.

Sult Arty Grünerløkka landmark specializing in simple, fresh cooking, with a menu that changes daily. 26 Thorvald Meyers Gate, Oslo; 47-2/287-0467; dinner for two ❙❙❙.

WHAT TO SEE & DO

National Theater The country's oldest permanent performing arts venue, and a popular summer hangout. 1 Engen, Bergen; 47-5/554-9700; dns.no.

Oslo Opera House Monumental structure by Norwegian design firm Snøhetta, who also designed Egypt's Bibliotheca Alexandrina. 1 Kirsten Flagstads Plass, Oslo; 47-2/142-2100; operaen.no.

BALTIC COAST

WHERE TO STAY & EAT

Baltic Beach Hotel White wedding cake–like building overlooking forest and sea. 23/25 Juras St., Majori, Jurmala, Latvia; 371-67/771-400; balticbeach.lv; doubles from $$.

Pädaste Manor Landscaped grounds along a protected shoreline, with a Magic Mountain–like spa. The restaurant, Sea House, has heavy stone walls and a meat-centric menu. Muhu, Estonia; 372/454-8800; padaste.ee; doubles from $$; dinner for two ⑂⑂⑂.

KRAKÓW

WHERE TO STAY
Hotel Amadeus 16th-century townhouse near Market Square. 20 Mikolajska; 48-12/429-6070; hotel-amadeus.pl; doubles from $$.
Karmel Hotel Cozy former tenement in the old Jewish district. 15 Kupa; 48-12/430-6697; karmel.com.pl; doubles from $.

WHERE TO EAT
Copernicus Polish classics gone upscale. 16 Ul. Kanonicza; 48-12/424-3421; hotel.com.pl; dinner for two ⑂⑂⑂.

NIGHTLIFE
Klub Kulturalny Down a short cobblestoned alleyway; known for its flavored vodkas—cherry, honey, or herb. 25 Ul. Szewska; 48-12/429-6739.
Moment Café Leather booth tables and a long cocktail menu. 34 Ul. Jozefa; 48-66/803-4000.
Pauza Nightspot that combines a gallery, club, and lounge. 18/3 Ul. Florianska; 48-60/263-7833.
Singer Café Funky spot with a speakeasy feel. 20 Ul. Estery; 48-12/292-0622.
Zblizenia Glossy and well-lit, for a stylish crowd. 7 1/2 Pl. Nowy; 48-12/430-0138.

ST. PETERSBURG

WHERE TO STAY
Taleon Imperial Hotel Restored czarist-era palace. 59 Moika River Emb.; 7-812/324-9911; eliseevpalacehotel.com; doubles from $$$.
Grand Hotel Europe St. Petersburg at its most sumptuous; past guests include a honeymooning Tchaikovsky. 1/7 Ul. Mikhailovskaya; 800/237-1236 or 7-812/329-6000; grandhoteleurope.com; doubles from $$$.

WHERE TO EAT
Restoran Modern twist on Russian classics, in a refreshingly simple dining room. 2 Tamozhenny Per.; 7-812/327-8979; dinner for two ⑂⑂⑂.
Terrassa Asian fare and a glass-enclosed balcony overlooking Nevsky Prospekt. 3 Ul. Kazanskaya; 7-812/337-6837; dinner for two ⑂⑂⑂.

WHAT TO SEE & DO
Church of our Savior on Spilled Blood Cathedral built on the site of Czar Alexander II's 1881 assassination. 26 Griboedova Kanala; 7-812/315-1636.
Mariinsky Theater The place for Russian ballet and opera; also home to a striking new concert hall. 1 Teatralnaya Ploshchad; 7-812/326-4141; mariinsky.ru.
State Hermitage Museum One of the world's oldest museums; six buildings (including the Winter Palace) that house more than 3 million works of art. 34 Dvortsovaya Embankment; 7-812/710-9625; hermitagemuseum.org.
Summer Palace Peter the Great's former residence, surrounded by gardens. Kutuzova Naberezhnaya 2.

WHERE TO SHOP
Imperial Porcelain Manufactory Outfitting the homes of Russian aristocracy since 1744. 151 Obukhovskoy Oborony Prospekt, and five other locations; 7-812/326-1744.

MOSCOW

WHERE TO STAY
MaMaison Pokrovka Suite Hotel Bright, geometric kitchenette-equipped suites with homey touches like four-poster beds. 40 Ul. Pokrovka; 7-495/229-5797; pokrovka-moscow.com; doubles from $$$.
Ritz-Carlton Modern luxury next to the Kremlin and Red Square. 3 Ul. Tverskaya; 7-495/225-8888; ritzcarlton.com; doubles from $$$$.

WHERE TO EAT
Barashka Azeri specialties, including Caspian sturgeon kebabs and herbaceous lamb stews. 21/1 Novy Arbat; 7-495/228-3731; dinner for two ⑂⑂.
Bosco Bar Pastas and salads alongside Russian classics like dacha-style fried potatoes. 3 Red Square; 7-495/627-3703; dinner for two ⑂⑂.
Genatsvale Arbat Georgian dishes like *khinkali* dumplings and chicken *satsivi*. 11/2 Novy Arbat; 7-495/697-9431; dinner for two ⑂⑂⑂.
Konditerskaya Pushkin Café Pushkin's ornate pastry annex. 26/5 Tverskoi Bul.; 7-495/6044280.
Nedalny Vostok Asian-inspired fare from Moscow's ruling restaurateur, Arkady Novikov. 15/2 Tverskoi Bul.; 7-495/694-0641; dinner for two ⑂⑂⑂.
Shinok Ukrainian cuisine in a recreated farmhouse. 2 Ul. 1905 Goda; 7-495/651-8101; dinner for two ⑂⑂⑂.
Stolovaya No. 57 Stalin-era staples in a replica of a Communist-era workers' canteen. At GUM department store, 3 Red Square; 7-495/788-4343; dinner for two ⑂.
Turandot Over-the-top restaurant palace crammed with chinoiserie, frescoes, and damask, serving fanciful fusion. 26/5 Tverskoy Bul.; 7-495/739-0011; dinner for two ⑂⑂⑂.

ISTANBUL

WHERE TO STAY
Hotel Poem Cozy, affordable option in the historic Sultanahmet district. 12 Terbiyik Sk.; 90-212/638-9744; hotelpoem.com; doubles from $.
Marmara Pera Centrally located high-rise with huge windows that look out over the city. Mesrutiyet Cad.; 90-212/251-4646; the marmarahotels.com; doubles from $$.

WHERE TO EAT
Babylon Lounge Burgers, pizza, and Mediterranean salads make a perfect post-concert meal. 4 Jurnal Sk.; 90-212/245-3800; dinner for two ⑂⑂.
Otto Wood-fired pizza shop that doubles as a dance club. 22 Sofyali Sk.; 90-212/252-6588; dinner for two ⑂⑂.

WHERE TO SHOP
Ümit Ünal Doors Young designer favored by Istanbul's fashionable set. 1B Ensiz Sk.; 90-212/245-7886.

NIGHTLIFE
Babylon Leading music venue that has hosted international names as well as local talent. 3 Sehbender Sk.; 90-212/292-7368.

LODGING   under $150 → $ $150—$299 → $$ $300—$699 → $$$ $700—$999 → $$$$ $1,000 + up → $$$$$

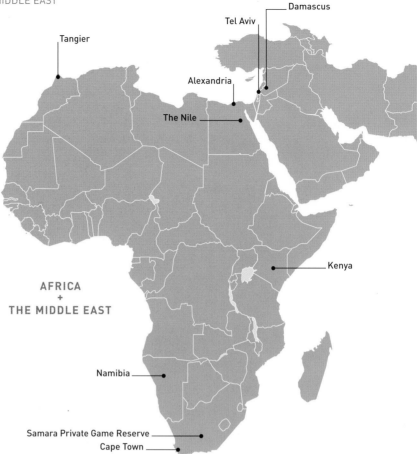

Tangier

Damascus

Tel Aviv

Alexandria

The Nile

AFRICA
+
THE MIDDLE EAST

Kenya

Namibia

Samara Private Game Reserve

Cape Town

AFRICA + THE MIDDLE EAST

TANGIER, MOROCCO

WHERE TO STAY

Hôtel Nord-Pinus Tanger
Set in an 18th-century pasha palace. 11 Rue du Riad Sultan; 212-661/228-140; nord-pinus-tanger.com; doubles from **$$**, including some meals and transfers.

WHERE TO EAT

Casa Garcia Laid-back restaurant frequented by artists and intellectuals, in the resort town of Asilah, an hour away from Tangier. 51

rue Moulay Hassan Ben el Mehdi, Asilah; 212-39/417-465; lunch for two ❚❚.

WHERE TO SHOP

Boutique Majid Centuries' worth of local goods piled high in a seemingly endless warren of rooms that might bring Ali Baba's cavern to mind. 66 Rue les Almou-hades; 212-539/938-892.
Boutique Volubilis For colorful booties and other accessories. 15 Petit Socco; 212-539/931-362.
Coin de L'Art Berbère Moroccan carpets, many priced below $300. 53 Rue les Almouhades; 212-539/938-094.
Fondouk Chejra Weavers' market full of bright and patterned textiles. Marché des Pauvres bldg., first

floor; Rue de la Liberté; no phone.
Galerie Tindouf Crammed with antiques. 72 Rue de la Liberté; 212-39/938-600.
Marrakech La Rouge In an inauspicious setting, quality items from all over Morocco: spice holders, hand-painted cups from Fez, inlaid boxes, and more. 50 Rue du 6 Avril; 212-539/931-117

KENYA

WHERE TO STAY
Lemarti's Camp
On the Uaso Nyiro River, five tents decorated with exqui-site African-themed *objets d'art* (from beaded walking sticks to crocodile skulls), in a verdant setting of scented

acacia trees. Run by Nairobi-based fashion designer Anna Trzebinski and her husband, Loyapan Lemarti. Koija, Laikipia; 212/568-7639; lemartis camp.com or journeysby design.co.uk; doubles from **$$$$$**, all-inclusive.
Ol Malo Four guest cottages and a six-bedroom villa on a 5,000-acre ranch. Nanyuki; 212/568-7639; olmalo.com or journeysbydesign.co.uk; doubles from **$$$$$**, all-inclusive.

NAMIBIA

WHERE TO STAY
Fort on Fisher's Pan
Moorish-inspired lodge on the southern edge of Etosha National Park, with North

African chandeliers and brass-tray bedside tables that exude casbah cool. 264-61/232-009; onguma. com; doubles from $$$$, all-inclusive.

Little Kulala The newest of three lodges in the Kulala Wilderness Reserve. wilderness-safaris.com; doubles from $$$$, all-inclusive.

Little Ongava Three cottages on the Ongava Game Reserve. wilderness-safaris.com; doubles from $$$$$, all-inclusive.

Serra Cafema Camp Eight chalets with private decks in Namibia's northwest corner. wilderness-safaris. com; doubles from $$$$, all-inclusive.

CAPE TOWN, SOUTH AFRICA

WHERE TO STAY

Cape Grace The city's most luxurious hotel; recently revamped rooms have Cape Dutch antiques and hand-painted fabrics in blues and creams. West Quay Rd., Victoria & Alfred Waterfront; 27-21/410-7100; capegrace. com; doubles from $$$.

Grand Daddy Hotel Playful new property with a penthouse Airstream trailer park decked in various themes (think The Ballad of John and Yoko, or Goldilocks and the 3 Bears). 38 Long St.; 27-21/424-7247; daddylonglegs.co.za; doubles from $.

WHERE TO EAT

Brewers & Union Sleek beer salon serving premium brews, cured meats, and artisanal cheeses. 110 Bree St., Heritage Square; 27-21/422-2770; drinks for two $.

Caveau Wine Bar & Deli Courtyard café; popular with the artistic set. 92 Bree St., Heritage Square; 27-21/422-1367; drinks for two $.

WHAT TO SEE & DO

Whatiftheworld Gallery Nexus for the city's emerging talent. 208 Albert Rd.; 27-21/448-1438; whatiftheworld.com.

WHERE TO SHOP

Clementina Ceramics Showroom of contemporary South African ceramicists and other artists. Old Biscuit Mill, 373–375 Albert Rd.; 27-21/447-1398.

Neighbourgoods Market Open-air stalls selling food, handmade goods, and designer pieces. Old Biscuit Mill, 373–375 Albert Rd.; neighbourgoods market.co.za.

SAMARA PRIVATE GAME RESERVE, SOUTH AFRICA

WHERE TO STAY

Karoo Lodge Colonial-era farmstead. Graaf-Reinet; 27-49/891-0880; samara. co.za; doubles from $$$, all-inclusive.

ALEXANDRIA, EGYPT

WHERE TO STAY

Four Seasons Hotel Alexandria at San Stefano The city's most luxurious hotel. 399 El Geish Rd.; 800/332-3442 or 20-3/581-8000; fourseasons.com; doubles from $$$.

Sofitel Cecil The setting for much of Lawrence Durrell's Alexandria Quartet novels; many rooms overlook the Mediterranean Sea. 16 Saad Zaghloul Square; 800/763-4835; 20-3/487-7173; sofitel. com; doubles from $$.

WHAT TO SEE & DO

Bibliotheca Alexandrina Glass-and-concrete library and cultural institutions on the city's waterfront. El Shatby; 20-3/483-9999; bibalex.org.

THE NILE, EGYPT

WHERE TO STAY

Sofitel Winter Palace Luxor Nineteenth-century property overlooking the Nile, near the temple of Luxor. Corniche el Nil; 800/763-4835 or 20-95/238-0425; doubles from $$.

Hotel al Moudira On 10 acres, with hammam-like bathrooms. Hager Al Dabbeya, West Bank, Luxor; 20-123/251-307; moudira. com; doubles from $$.

CRUISING

Sudan Built in 1885, with recently revamped cabins; the sundeck is the best spot from which to watch the shore's changing scenery. www.steam-ship-sudan. com; four-day cruise from $$$$$, based on double occupancy.

TEL AVIV, ISRAEL

WHERE TO STAY

Cinema Hotel Bauhaus-style building that was one of the first movie theaters in the city. 1 Zamenhoff St.; 972-3/520-7100; cinema hotel.com; doubles from $$.

Hotel Montefiore New 12-room boutique property. 36 Montefiore St.; 972-3/564-6100; doubles from $$$.

WHAT TO SEE & DO

Bauhaus Foundation Museum Original pieces by Bauhaus masters. 21 Bialik St.; 972-3/620-4664.

NIGHTLIFE

Shalvata Waterfront bar and restaurant in the converted port district. Near Hangar 25; 972-3/544-1279.

DAMASCUS, SYRIA

WHERE TO STAY

Beit al Mamlouka Eight bedrooms in a gloriously renovated 17th-century home. al-Qaimariyya Street, Old City; 963-11/543-0445; almamlouka.com; doubles from $$.

Talisman Romantic 17-room retreat in the Jewish Quarter. 116 Tal el-Hijara Street, Old City; 963-11/541-5379; hoteltalisman.net; doubles from $$.

WHERE TO EAT

Al-Kamal Old World restaurant with regional and home-style specials. 29 Mai St.; 963-11/232-3572; dinner for two from ↑↑.

Bekdach Popular ice cream with an elastic texture, rolled with crushed pistachios. In the Souq al-Hamadiyeh.

WHAT TO SEE & DO

Beit Farhi Currently being restored as a boutique hotel, a former residence in the city's Jewish quarter. Off al-Amin St.

Hammam Bakry Ottoman-era bathhouse with separate hours for men and women. Bakry Lane, Bab Touma, Old City; 63-11/542-6606.

Umayyad Mosque Site weighted with historic, religious, and architectural significance; one of Islam's first great mosques. Entrance at the northern Bab al-Amara gate.

ASIA

Tokyo
Shizuoka
Seoul
Lhasa
Yunnan
Delhi
Maheshwar
Palawan
Bangkok
Pranburi
Langkawi
Saigon
Bali

ASIA

TOKYO

WHERE TO STAY
Ginza Yoshimizu Eleven rooms on 10 floors; a modern take on a traditional Japanese *ryokan*. 3-11-3 Ginza, Chuo-ku; 81-3/3248-4432; yoshimizu.com; doubles from **$$**.

Mandarin Oriental Tokyo Hushed public areas complement understated rooms with the latest technological amenities. 2-1-1 Nihonbashi Muromachi, Chuo-ku; 800/526-6566 or 81-3/3270-8800; mandarinoriental. com; doubles from **$$$**.

WHERE TO EAT
Buri Bar and lounge serving sakes from all over Japan. 1-14-1 Ebisu Nishi, Shibuya-ku; 81-3/3496-7744; dinner for two ❙❙.

Butagumi Pork with a Ph.D. 2-24-9 Nishi-Azabu, Minato-ku; 81-3/5466-6775; dinner for two ❙❙❙❙.

Gyoza Stadium and Ice Cream Stadium Masses of food vendors and an entire floor devoted to ice cream. Namco Namja Town, second and third floors, Sunshine City, Higashi-Ikebukuro 3 cho-me, Toshima-ku; 81-3/5950-0765; lunch for two ❙.

Patisserie Sadaharu Aoki Delicately flavored, design-worthy pastries. Shinkoku-sai Building, first floor, 3-4-1 Marunouchi, Chiyoda-ku; 81-3/5293-2800.

Patisserie Satsuki Pastries with international themes. New Otani Hotel, 4-1 Kioi-cho, Chiyoda-ku; 81-3/3221-7252.

Takashimaya Times Square The basement food hall has more than 100 purveyors. 5-24-2 Sendagaya, Shibuya-ku; 81-3/5361-1111.

SHIZUOKA, JAPAN

WHERE TO STAY
Arai Ryokan Traditional Japanese inn and hot springs; rooms have beautifully framed views of gardens and maple-shaded carp ponds. 970 Shuzenji, Izu, Shizuoka, 81-558/722-007; arairyokan.net; doubles from **$$**, including meals.

SEOUL

WHERE TO STAY
Park Hyatt Seoul The city's largest guest rooms, with floor-to-ceiling windows and deep-soaking tubs. 995-14 Daechi-dong, Gangnam-gu; 82-2/2016-1234; hyatt.com; doubles from **$$**.

Shilla Seoul Contemporary slope-side hotel a bit removed from the center of town. 202 Jangchung-dong 2-ga, Jung-gu; 82-2/2233-3131; shilla.net; doubles from **$$$**.

WHERE TO EAT & DRINK
Bar Da Atmospheric dive. 365-12 Seogyo-dong, Mapu-gu; 82-2/334-5572; drinks for two **$**.

Budnamujip Known for its *galbi*, or short ribs, which are cut off the bone with a jeweler's precision. 1340-5 Seocho-dong, Seocho-gu; 82-2/3473-4167; dinner for two ❙❙.

Solmoemaeul Airy restaurant with traditional multicourse menus. 62 Samcheong-dong, Jongno-gu; 82-2/720-0995; dinner for two ❙❙.

WHAT TO SEE & DO
Kyobo Bookstore Three locations in Seoul, including the sprawling Gwanghwamun branch. Jogno 1-ga; 82-2/3704-2000.

Leeum, Samsung Museum of Art Korean works, from traditional to contemporary, in three architecturally significant structures. 747-18 Hannam-dong, Yongsan-gu; 82-2/2014-6900; leeum. samsungfoundation.org.

Lotte World Indoor and outdoor amusement park, sports center, and shopping complex. 40-1, Jamsil-Dong, Songpa-Gu; 82-2/411-2000.

War Memorial of Korea One of the biggest war museums in the world. 8 Yongsan-dong 1-ga, Yongsan-gu; 82-2/709-3139; warmemo.co.kr.

Yongsan Electronics Market Five thousand stores selling appliances and gadgets at discounted prices. 15-2 Hangangno 3-ga, Yongsan-gu.

YUNNAN, CHINA

WHERE TO STAY
Wenhai Ecolodge Guesthouse collective built in traditional Naxi style and run by locals. Wenhai village, Baisha Township,

🍴 DINING   under $25 →❙ $25–$74 →❙❙ $75–$149 →❙❙❙ $150–$299 →❙❙❙❙ $300 + up →❙❙❙❙❙

Yulong County, Lijiang; 86-139/0888-1817; northwest yunnan.com; doubles from $.

TOURS

Lijiang Xintuo Ecotourism Company Arranges transportation and itineraries with meals and accommodations (which could include homestays with a local family). 86-88/8510-6226; ecotourism.com.cn; from $$$ for four nights, all-inclusive.

LHASA, TIBET

WHERE TO STAY

Tangula Custom-built luxury train with a multiday route across the tundra from Beijing to Lhasa. 86-10/5809-5333; tangula luxurytrains.com; from $$$$.

Brahmaputra Grand Hotel Traditional decor with old artifacts. 86-891/630-9999; Tower B, Yangcheng Plaza, Gongbutang Rd.; doubles from $.

Yak Hotel Lhasa favorite in the old quarter, walking distance from the Jokhang Temple. 86-891/632-3496; 100 Beijing East Rd.; doubles from $.

WHAT TO SEE & DO

Potala Palace Citadel of the Dalai Lamas. Off Dekyi Shar Lam in eastern Lhasa.

Jokhang Temple Tibet's most revered religious structure. Between Dekyi Shar Lam and Chingdröl Shar Lam (Jiangsu Lu).

SAIGON (HO CHI MINH CITY)

WHERE TO STAY

Caravelle Hotel Runner-up to the Park Hyatt Saigon for the title of the city's best hotel. 19 Lam Son Square; 84-8/3823-4999; caravelle hotel.com; doubles from $$.

Park Hyatt Saigon Two stellar restaurants, a fine spa, an enviable location, and assured service. 2 Lam Son Square; 888/591-1234 or 84-8/3824-1234; hyatt.com; doubles from $$$.

WHERE TO EAT

Quan An Ngon Classic sidewalk dishes, including *bun cha gio* (rice vermicelli with fresh herbs and crispy spring rolls). 138 Nam Ky Khoi Nghia St.; 84-8/3825-7179; dinner for two ¶.

Temple Club Beautifully designed bar-restaurant with Art Deco details and sultry Indochine ambiance, plus a very good *mi quang* soup. 29–31 Ton That Thiep St.; 84-8/3829-9244; dinner for two ¶¶.

Xu Snazzy restaurant, cafe, and lounge (run by a Vietnamese-Australian) dishing out upmarket versions of local favorites. 71–75 Hai Ba Trung St., level 1; 84-8/3824-8469; lunch for two ¶.

WHERE TO SHOP

Saigon Kitsch and Dogma Gallery Looking for a keychain emblazoned with North Vietnamese tanks or a wartime propaganda poster? This delightful shop and gallery is your place. 43 Ton That Thiep St.; dogma vietnam.com; 84-8/3821-8019 or 84-8/3911-0986.

PALAWAN, PHILIPPINES

WHERE TO STAY

El Nido Beach Hotel Clean, bright, modern, and comfortable—a refreshing alternative to the island's rustic guesthouses. Hama St., El Nido; 63-48/723-0887; elnidobeachhotel.com; doubles from $.

Miniloc Island Resort Whitewashed overwater cabins with thatch roofs, as well as garden and hillside cottages. 63-2/894-5644; elnidoresorts.com; doubles from $$.

BALI, INDONESIA

WHERE TO STAY

Anantara Seminyak Resort & Spa Blends minimalism with traditional Balinese architecture; suites are equipped with Jacuzzis on private terraces. Jalan Dhyana Pura, Seminyak; 62-361/737-773; bali.anantara.com; doubles from $$.

Four Seasons Resort Bali at Sayan Forty-two freestanding villas, each with a plunge pool, plus 18 suites and one of the island's best spas. Gianyar; 800/332-3442 or 62-361/977-577; fourseasons.com; doubles from $$.

WHAT TO SEE & DO

Pura Besakih On the slopes of Mount Agung, the most important temple complex in Bali.

DELHI

WHERE TO STAY

The Imperial Art Deco icon with a Raj-era collection, clubby bar, and neatly clipped lawns. Janpath, New Delhi; 91-11/2334-1234; theimperialindia.com; doubles from $$$.

Oberoi, New Delhi The city's top business hotel, overlooking a golf course and Humayun's Tomb. Dr. Zakir Hussain Marg, New Delhi; 800/528-6088 or 91-11/2436-3030; oberoidelhi.com; doubles from $$.

WHERE TO EAT

Threesixty° Dazzling interiors and an extensive menu: from sushi and yakitori to a knockout butter chicken. In the Oberoi Hotel. Dr. Zakir Hussain Marg, New Delhi; 91-11/2436-3030; dinner for two ¶¶¶.

WHAT TO SEE & DO

Humayun's Tomb Splendid 16th-century Mughal monument that was an architectural forerunner of the Taj Mahal. Nizamuddin, New Delhi.

Nizamuddin Mosque Qawwali singers perform every Friday evening at this Sufi shrine and temple complex, not far from Humayun's Tomb (ask your concierge to arrange for a driver and guide). Nizamuddin, New Delhi.

Lodi Garden The green heart of New Delhi; a favorite of bird-watchers, picnicking families, and strolling couples.

NIGHTLIFE

Olive Beach Enormously popular bar-restaurant where Bollywood starlets sip top-shelf caipiroskas till 1 a.m. Hotel Diplomat, 9 Sardar Patel Marg, Chanakyapuri, New Delhi; 91-11/4604-0404; drinks for two ¶.

MAHESHWAR, INDIA

WHERE TO STAY

Ahilya Fort High above the Narmada River, 14 rooms within 18th-century battlements. Ahilya Wada, Maheshwar, Indore, Madhya Pradesh; 91-11/4155-1575;

ahilyafort.com; doubles from $$$, all-inclusive; two-night minimum.

WHERE TO SHOP
Rehwa Society Hand-loomed saris, scarves, shawls, and yard goods at startlingly reasonable prices, sold at a small shop at Ahilya Fort.

BANGKOK

WHERE TO STAY
The Eugenia Twelve suites in a faux-colonial mansion, with copper-plated bathtubs and numerous antiques. 267 Sukhumvit Soi 31; 66-2/259-9011; theeugenia.com; doubles from $$.
Mandarin Oriental Riverside grande dame of Bangkok hotels. 48 Oriental Ave.; 800/526-6566 or 66-2/659-9000; mandarinoriental.com; doubles from $$$.

WHERE TO EAT
Som Tam Nua Isan food from Thailand's northeast region. 392/14 Siam Square Soi 5, off Rama I Rd.; 66-2/251-4880; dinner for two ⑂.

WHAT TO SEE & DO
Grand Palace Complex of state buildings, temples, and royal residences. Sana Chai Rd., Old City; 66-2/224-1833.
Siam Paragon Mall Gigantic shopping center with an aquarium, a bowling alley, and a concert hall. 991/1 Rama I Rd.; 66-2/690-1000.
Wat Suthat One of Bangkok's oldest temples, with a 26-foot-tall gilt Buddha statue. 146 Bamrung Muang Rd.; 66-2/222-0280.

NIGHTLIFE
Bed Supperclub Bangkok's beautiful people flock to this restaurant-lounge to hobnob on white beds.

26 Sukhumvit Soi 11; 66-2/651-3537.
Tapas Room Club DJs spin house and funk at this fashionable club off Silom Road. 114/17-18 Silom Soi 4; 66-2/234-4737.

PRANBURI, THAILAND

WHERE TO STAY
Brassiere Beach Soothing, blue- and white-hued rooms in a garden setting. 210 Moo 5, Tambon Samroiyod; 66-32/630-555; brassierebeach.com; doubles from $.
X2 Kui Buri Design-minded bungalows on a former coconut plantation next to unspoiled oceanfront. 52 Moo 13, Ao Noi, Muang; 66-26/968-239; x2resorts.com; doubles from $.

LANGKAWI, MALAYSIA

WHERE TO STAY
Bon Ton Resort Eight beautifully refurbished Malay wooden stilt houses, each with distinctive decor. Jalan Pantai Cenang; 60-4/955-1688; bontonresort.com.my; doubles from $.
The Datai Set amid virgin rain forest, fronting a pristine, secluded cove. Kedah, Langkawi; 60-4/959-2500; ghmhotels.com; doubles from $$$$.
Four Seasons Langkawi Teak-shingled villas look out over a sugar-sand beach and dramatic limestone formations that trail out to sea like strings of pearls. Jalan Tanjung Rhu, Langkawi; 800/332-3443 or 60-4/950-8888; fourseasons.com; doubles from $$.

AUSTRALIA + NEW ZEALAND + THE SOUTH PACIFIC

MELBOURNE

WHERE TO STAY
Crown Towers Glittering high-rise in the Crown Entertainment complex, with boutiques, restaurants, and a 24-hour casino. 8 Whiteman St.; 61-3/9292-6868; crowntowers.com.au; doubles from $$$$$.
The Langham, Melbourne Business-traveler favorite with views over the Yarra River. 1 Southgate Ave.; 800/745-8883 or 61-3/8696-8888; langhamhotels.com; doubles from $$$.

WHERE TO EAT
Bistro Guillaume Elegant French-inspired cooking from one of Australia's finest chefs. Crown Entertainment Complex, 8 Whiteman St.; 61-3/9693-3888; dinner for two ⑂⑂⑂.
Giuseppe, Arnaldo & Sons Casual and sleek, with rustic Italian fare and a no-reservations policy. Crown Entertainment Complex, 8 Whiteman St.; 61-3/9694-7400; dinner for two ⑂⑂⑂.
Rockpool Bar & Grill Beef that's dry-aged on the premises. Crown Entertainment Complex, 8 Whiteman St.; 61-3/8648-1900; dinner for two ⑂⑂⑂⑂.

NEW SOUTH WALES, AUSTRALIA

WHERE TO STAY
Bannisters Point Lodge Cliffside boutique hotel

above Mollymook Beach. 191 Mitchell Parade, Mollymook; 61-2/4455-3044; bannisters.com.au; doubles from $$.
Paperbark Camp Twelve luxury tents set in a forest of eucalyptus trees. 571 Woollamia Rd., Woollamia; 61-2/4441-6066; www.paperbarkcamp.com.au; doubles from $$.

WHERE TO EAT
Berry Sourdough Bakery & Café BYOB restaurant serving modern Australian cuisine. 23 Prince Alfred St., Berry; 61-2/4464-1617; dinner for two ⑂⑂.

WHAT TO SEE & DO
Fo Guang Shan Nan Tien Temple The Southern Hemisphere's largest Buddhist temple. Berkeley Rd., Berkeley; 61-2/4272-0600.
Murramarang National Park Thirty thousand protected acres are home to kangaroos and parrots. Off Princes Hwy. at East Lynne; 61-2/4478-6582.

FAR NORTH QUEENSLAND, AUSTRALIA

WHERE TO STAY
Rose Gums Wilderness Retreat Nine kitted-out pole-and-timber tree houses, about an hour and a half from Cairns. Land Rd., via Lake Eacham, Atherton Tablelands; 61-7/4096-8360; rosegums.com.au; doubles from $$.
Sebel Reef House & Spa Room-wide windows overlook the Coral Sea at this 69-room hotel with three pools and a spa. 99 Williams Esplanade, Palm Cove; 61-7/4055-3633; reefhouse.com.au; doubles from $$.

DINING under $25 →⑂ $25–$74 →⑂⑂ $75–$149 →⑂⑂⑂ $150–$299 →⑂⑂⑂⑂ $300 + up →⑂⑂⑂⑂⑂

The Top End

Far North Queensland

Marquesas Islands

Bora-Bora

New South Wales

Melbourne

**AUSTRALIA +
NEW ZEALAND
+ THE SOUTH
PACIFIC**

Southland

WHERE TO EAT

Nu Nu Restaurant One of Queensland's best spots for dining; stylish interiors and a menu that lists local purveyors. 123 Williams Esplanade, Palm Cove; 61-7/4059-1880; dinner for two ⫯⫯⫯.

Ochre Restaurant Known for its superior (and sustainable) seafood. 43 Shields St., Cairns; 61-7/4051-0100; dinner for two ⫯⫯⫯.

Piccolo Cucina Specialties include pizzas and house-made pastas. 92a Lake St., Cairns; 61-7/4051-5137; dinner for two ⫯⫯⫯.

Twelve Bar Café Breakfast means free-range eggs and yogurt from a biodynamic farm. Corner of Lake and Shields Streets, Cairns; 61-7/4031-2912; breakfast for two ⫯.

WHAT TO SEE & DO

Coffee Works Sample the joe and chocolates, then check out the museum— a collection of quirky coffee paraphernalia. 136 Mason St., Mareeba; 61-7/4092-4101.

Skybury Tours and tastings at Australia's oldest coffee plantation. Ivicevic Rd., Mareeba; 61-7/4093-2194.

WHERE TO SHOP

Rusty's Market Exotic fruit, fresh fish, and handmade pasta are sold at this all-encompassing bazaar. Grafton and Sheridan Streets; 61-7/4051-5100.

Vannella Cheese Factory Run by the Minoia family (transplants from Puglia) and famous for its buffalo mozzarella. 18 Hollingsworth St., Bungalow; 61-7/4035-1766.

THE TOP END, AUSTRALIA

WHERE TO STAY

Bamurru Plains Overlooking the Mary River floodplain, nine open-plan safari tents surrounded by wildlife. Swim Creek Station, near Point Stuart, Northern Territory; 61-2/9571-6399; bamurruplains.com; doubles from $$$$, all-inclusive.

Home Valley Station Sprawling cattle ranch with accommodations that range from canvas tents to well-appointed "grass castles." Gibb River Rd., East Kimberley, Western Australia; 61-8/9161-4322; homevalley.com.au; doubles from $.

WHAT TO SEE & DO

Waringarri Aboriginal Arts Studio Where native painters interpret their "Dreaming" stories on canvas. Speargrass Rd., opposite Kelley's Knob, Western Australia; 61-8/9168-2212; waringarriarts.com.au.

Warmun Roadhouse Fuel, fish-and-chips, a general store, and a post office, near the entrance to Purnululu National Park. Lot 22, Great Northern Hwy., Kununurra, Western Australia; 61-8/9168-7882; warmunroadhouse.com.au.

SOUTHLAND, NEW ZEALAND

WHERE TO STAY

Fiordland Lodge Ten-room main building and two log cabins. 472 Te Anau Milford Hwy.; 64-3/249-7832; fiordlandlodge.co.nz, doubles from $$$.

The Lodge at Tikana Ultra-private country retreat with a 100-acre farm. 374 Livingstone Rd., Winton; 64-3/236-4117; tikana.co.nz; doubles from $$$$.

Mandeno House Modern B&B just steps away from Dunedin's restaurants, museums, and botanical gardens. 667 George St., Dunedin; 64-3/471-9595; mandenohouse.com; doubles from $$.

BORA-BORA

WHERE TO STAY

Four Seasons Resort Bora Bora On a glorious white-sand beach; eight of the bungalows have individual plunge pools and views of Mount Otemanu. Motu Tehotu; 800/332-3442 or 689/603-130; fourseasons.com; bungalows from $$$$.

Novotel Bora Bora Beach Resort Good-value accommodation on Matira Beach, with an in-house dive center. 800/515-5679 or 689/605-950; accorhotels.com; doubles from $$.

WHERE TO EAT

Villa Mahana Exclusive restaurant with an island-inspired menu. 689/675-063; dinner for two ⫯⫯⫯⫯⫯.

THE MARQUESAS ISLANDS

WHERE TO STAY

Hiva Oa Hanakee Pearl Lodge Fourteen bungalows facing Tehueto Valley and an open ocean channel. 800/657-3275 or 689/508-452; pearlresorts.com; doubles from $$$.

WHAT TO SEE & DO

Paul Gauguin Cultural Center Spot-on reproductions of Gaugin's work, in a homegrown museum built to coincide with the 100th anniversary of the artist's death. Atuona; 689/927-897.

INDEX

TRIPS DIRECTORY

CONTRIBUTORS

Gini Alhadeff

Richard Alleman

Kurt Andersen

Katie Arnold

Tom Austin

Luke Barr

Laura Begley

Thomas Beller

John Berendt

Mary Bianco

Anya von Bremzen

John Brennan

Michael Cain

Jennifer Chen

Jennifer Conlin

Christopher R. Cox

Justin Davidson

Hadas Dembo

Anthony Dennis

Joe Dolce

Simon Doonan

Mary Tonetti Dorra

Robyn Eckhardt

Ursula Fousler

Candice Gianetti

Michael Gross

Darrell Hartman

James Patrick Herman

Deniz Huysal

Sarah Kantrowitz

Megan Kaplan

David Kaufman

David A. Keeps

Brad Kessler

Leanne Kitchen

Chris Kucway

Matt and Ted Lee

Peter Jon Lindberg

M. G. Lord

Heather Smith MacIsaac

Jane Margolies

Francine Maroukian

Alexandra Marshall

Shane Mitchell

Ian Mount

Sean Rocha

Michael Rowe

Julian Rubinstein

Joanna Savill

Bruce Schoenfeld

Clara Sedlak

Josh Sens

Maria Shollenbarger

Gary Shteyngart

Adam Skolnick

Scott Spencer

Jeff Spurrier

David Stern

Simon Thomsen

Guy Trebay

Meeghan Truelove

Alison Tyler

Pia Ulin

Valerie Waterhouse

Susan Welsh

Nina Willdorf

Jeff Wise

Michael Z. Wise

Stephanie Wood

Lynn Yaeger

Most of the stories in this book first appeared in *Travel + Leisure* magazine, and have been updated and adapted for use here. To learn more about these destinations, or to read the original stories, go to travelandleisure.com.

On the beach in Pranburi, Thailand.

PHOTOGRAPHERS

A magazine of modern global culture, *Travel + Leisure* examines the places, ideas, and trends that define the way we travel now. T+L inspires readers to explore the world, equipping them with expert advice and a better understanding of the endless possibilities of travel. Delivering clear, comprehensive service journalism, intelligent writing, and evocative photography, T+L is the authority for today's traveler. Visit us at **travelandleisure.com.**